Between the Ice

POETS ON POETRY

David Lehman, General Editor
Donald Hall, Founding Editor

New titles

William Logan, *All the Rage*
Anne Stevenson, *Between the Iceberg and the Ship*
C. K. Williams, *Poetry and Consciousness*

Recently published

Allen Grossman, *The Long Schoolroom*
Jonathan Holden, *Guns and Boyhood in America*
Andrew Hudgins, *The Glass Anvil*
Josephine Jacobsen, *The Instant of Knowing*
Carol Muske, *Women and Poetry*
Charles Simic, *Orphan Factory*
William Stafford, *Crossing Unmarked Snow*
May Swenson, *Made with Words*

Also available are collections by

A. R. Ammons, Robert Bly, Philip Booth, Marianne Boruch,
Hayden Carruth, Fred Chappell, Amy Clampitt, Tom Clark,
Douglas Crase, Robert Creeley, Donald Davie, Peter Davison,
Tess Gallagher, Suzanne Gardinier, Thom Gunn, John Haines,
Donald Hall, Joy Harjo, Robert Hayden, Daniel Hoffman,
Weldon Kees, Galway Kinnell, Mary Kinzie, Kenneth Koch,
Richard Kostelanetz, Maxine Kumin, Martin Lammon (editor),
David Lehman, Philip Levine, John Logan, William Matthews,
William Meredith, Jane Miller, John Frederick Nims, Gregory Orr,
Alicia Ostriker, Marge Piercy, Anne Sexton, Charles Simic,
Louis Simpson, William Stafford, Richard Tillinghast,
Diane Wakoski, Alan Williamson, Charles Wright, and
James Wright

Anne Stevenson

Between the Iceberg and the Ship

SELECTED ESSAYS

Ann Arbor
THE UNIVERSITY OF MICHIGAN PRESS

*To the historian Mark Elvin
who taught me to walk warily in Label Land.*

Copyright © by the University of Michigan 1998
All rights reserved
Published in the United States of America by
The University of Michigan Press
Manufactured in the United States of America
♾ Printed on acid-free paper

2001   2000   1999   1998   4 3 2 1

A CIP catalog record for this book is available from the British Library.

Library of Congress Cataloging-in-Publication Data

Stevenson, Anne, 1933 Jan. 3–
    Between the iceberg and the ship : selected essays / Anne
Stevenson.
        p.   cm. — (Poets on poetry)
    Includes bibliographical references (p.   ).
    ISBN 0-472-09645-1 (cloth : alk. paper). — ISBN 0-472-06645-5
(pbk. : alk. paper)
    1. Stevenson, Anne, 1933 Jan. 3– —Aesthetics.   2. Ireland—In
literature.   3. Poetics.   I. Title.   II. Series.
PR6069.T45B48   1998
824'.914—dc21   98-19832
                                                          CIP

Preface

We'd rather have the iceberg than the ship
although it meant the end of travel . . .
                                    —Elizabeth Bishop

The articles and lectures in this book have been arranged according to a few themes or arguments running through them. The first essay, "Writing as a Woman," happens also to be the earliest; it goes back to 1977. The final interview with Richard Poole was completed—by letter—late in 1995, although I have since slightly revised my part in it.

All the essays are personal. Most were written on request or in answer to specific questions; some are simply prose amplifications of poems. They form a record of one person's engagement with poetry over twenty years, but they don't, for me, represent either an American or a British perspective. They speak, rather, from the viewpoint of someone who stands at a remove from the academic profession in both countries, trying to make a place for poetry without either politicizing it or rendering it sterile through overanalysis.

I am grateful to the following editors, publishers, journals, and individuals for permission to reprint copyright materials: Ted Hughes and the Estate of Sylvia Plath, Faber and Faber Ltd, and HarperCollins Publishers for "Natural History" from *Collected Poems* by Sylvia Plath (New York: HarperCollins, 1981); Faber and Faber Ltd and Alfred A. Knopf, Inc. for excerpts from *Collected Poems* by Wallace Stevens; AP Watt Ltd, on behalf of the Trustees of the Robert Graves Copyright Trust, for "A Cool Web" from *Collected Poems* by Robert Graves; Faber and Faber Ltd and Harcourt Brace for excerpts from poems by T. S. Eliot; David Higham Associates for "House on a Cliff" by Louis MacNeice; Sophie Gurney and Elisabeth Hanbro for an extract from Gwen Raverat's *Period Piece;* and Magda Salvesen for an extract from *The Sound of Sleat* by Jon Shueler.

Contents

I

Writing as a Woman

Writing as a Woman

Suppose we begin by calling to mind some scenes from Sylvia Plath's *The Bell Jar*. Esther Greenwood, a heroine who more obviously than most is a version of the author, has returned from a disillusioning experience as a student editor of a ladies' magazine in New York. The glamorous world of fashion writing and famous authors has proved to be a fraud. Her fellow students have been frivolous, the parties tedious; the men, vain or sadistic, have failed to seduce or even interest her. At the climactic dinner, crabmeat and avocado salad, roasted in photographer's lights, have laid the whole company flat with ptomaine poisoning. Finally, at the end of her stay, Esther stands on the parapet of her hotel feeding piece after piece of her fashionable wardrobe to the night winds—a gesture of anger and defiance so total that she is forced to barter her dressing gown for clothes to travel in the next day.

When Esther returns to her mother in suburban Westchester, the first thing she hears is that her application for a writers' course in Cambridge has been turned down. She has already seen through the shallow hypocrisy of her medical-student boyfriend, Buddy Willard, and his "clean-living" family. The summer has been a disaster in its first month, and Esther Greenwood, for the first time in the course of a stunningly successful adolescence, is forced to face up to what she is. What she is turns out to be a girl—a middle-class American girl, talented and ambitious, yes, but of whom things are expected that have nothing to do with her talents and ambitions. Poor Esther. Poor Sylvia.

Now, I want to disregard, temporarily, Sylvia Plath's own psychological troubles (they have been too much discussed in any case) and look instead at the predicament of Esther Greenwood. What are we to say of this account in *The Bell Jar* of a talented woman's first brush with—we must call it for lack of a better term—"the real world"?

From *Women Writing and Women Writing about Women*, ed. Mary Jacobus (New York: Barnes and Noble Books, 1979).

If we are truly bigoted we can dismiss Esther's suffering as the neurosis of an "overachievement-oriented schoolgirl." But none of us would want to do that. More to the point, we can regard *The Bell Jar* as an honest, often brilliant, account of a woman's confrontation with a society many of whose values are an insult to her integrity. However, there is more to *The Bell Jar* than this. For as a writer, Esther Greenwood, like Sylvia Plath, has a vested interest *in* her society. She craves its approval and she needs it for material. She also has instinctive "womanly" feelings, and quite naturally she is curious about sex, babies, marriage, and what her future as a woman will be.

The trouble in *The Bell Jar* seems to be this: throughout most of her life Esther has pulled herself to the top of her society—at school, at college—by native intelligence and stupendous will-power. Now, suddenly, she finds that she is a victim of forces beyond her control . . . forces that are also desires. She wants to be a complete woman, but in most womanly roles she can't excel. Why can she not cook, take shorthand, dance, play the piano, translate languages, do all the things in the world women are expected to do to help men? And why, on the other hand, do the things she *can* do (write, win academic prizes, win scholar-ships) seem not to matter to other people, particularly men—or, if they do matter, lead to disillusionment? The editing job was a fiasco; the writing course wouldn't accept her.

These two streams of (seemingly) personal failure under-mine and finally paralyze her will. After a series of imaginary flights to other, quite impossible selves (she should marry a prison guard on Deer Island and have a parcel of kids; she should become a Catholic and confess to a priest; she should study shorthand, become a typist, be a waitress)—after these flights away from her own personality have come to nothing, Esther turns to the only refuge from her torment she can think of and attempts to kill herself in a corner under the house.

It is not my purpose to undertake an analysis of *The Bell Jar*, though I might point out that, as a piece of writing, the tough, amused bitterness of the first third of the book dissolves into jerky passages of confession and crude resentment once the breakdown has occurred. What is of interest to us, however, is that Sylvia Plath implies all the way through that the roles of "writer" and "woman" are in some way incompatible. Yet, like so many of us, she was damned if she herself was going to forgo one to become the other. The tension between the two roles—the woman and the writer—is a source of energy in her poems, but it is also, I think, a source of their self-destructiveness. What seems most self-destructive in Plath's work is a haunting fear of failure. The emotional power she summons from her subconscious is a mixture of a fear of inadequacy and a knowledge of her superiority. She establishes her astringently defiant tone in a language of inventive complaint and embattled anger.

I hasten to add that this mixture of inadequacy and superiority is common in American writing. It is to be found all through Berryman and Lowell, and even in Whitman. Since we are talking of women, it is of interest to note that Emily Dickinson's letters—when she was exercising her ferocious wit—make use of the same defiant tone that Sylvia Plath perfected in parts of *The Bell Jar*. Let's compare two passages. Here is Emily Dickinson describing her family to Colonel Higginson.

> I have Brother & a Sister—My Mother does not care for thought— and Father, too busy with his Briefs—to notice what we do. He buys me many Books—but begs me not to read them—because he fears they joggle the Mind. They are all religious-except-me and address an Eclipse, every morning,—whom they call their "Father."

Can you think of a more devastating attack on the male-dominated family than that? And yet, the wit is suspect. We know that Emily Dickinson adored her father, rather pitied as well as despised her mother, relied on her sister to make her way in the world possible. So her *real* attitude is defensive of the system she is attacking. What is wrong with her world is exactly what gives her advantages in it, as a woman and as a writer. She is superior in intelligence to everyone she knows, but inferior in ability to meet the world on *its* terms. She decides, therefore, quite early in her life that it will suit her better not to try. In her letters she makes fun of a state of affairs she could never have borne to change.

Sylvia Plath was, of course, temperamentally a different creature altogether. She wanted to be a good writer, but she also wanted to be an exceptionally efficient wife, mother, and housekeeper; we know that from the recently published *Letters Home*

(1975). Her attack on Dodo Conway, as Dodo pushes her creaking pram under Esther's window in the suburbs, is partly an attack on the general slovenlinesss of human beings when they allow themselves to go nature's way without the puritan constraints of self-control.

> A woman not five feet tall, with a grotesque protruding stomach, was wheeling an old black baby carriage down the street. Two or three small children of various sizes, all pale, with smudgy faces and bare smudgy knees, wobbled along in the shadow of her skirts.
> A serene, almost religious smile lit up the woman's face. Her head tilted happily back, like a sparrow egg perched on a duck egg, she smiled into the sun.

But like Emily Dickinson, Sylvia Plath is not showing her full hand. For (as Plath herself sees) Dodo Conway is a *happy* woman. She is far happier, with her babies and her protruding stomach, than Esther is, or Esther's mother, whose efforts to bring up two children to be clean-living, responsible citizens are in some ways more threatening to Esther's creativeness than Dodo's untidy brood. Dodo presents Esther with an alternative that a part of her wants to accept.

Having no father, Sylvia Plath cannot fondly make fun of him, as Emily Dickinson could of hers. You remember how in *The Bell Jar,* Plath has Esther make a pilgrimage to her father's grave, not to honor him but to blame him. She can never forgive him for dying and leaving her to the mercies of her mother. The language of this passage is too double-edged to be accidental, and it is in some ways a key to the book: "I had a great yearning, lately, to *pay my father back* for all the years of neglect, and start tending his grave" (my italics). Literally, "to pay back" means to pay back what she owes, to pay her debt to her father. But "to pay back" also means to take revenge. Esther is revenging herself for *his* neglect of *her* at the same time as she is apologizing for *her* neglect of *him*. Still, the relationship between daughter and dead father is more interesting and creative than that between daughter and living mother. The mother is presented in every instance as a despicable object; her goodness and devotion only annoy. There are moments when Esther wants to kill her.

The room blued into view, and I wondered where the night had gone. My mother turned from a foggy log into a slumbering, middle-aged woman, her mouth slightly open and a snore ravelling from her throat. The piggish noise irritated me, and for a while it seemed to me that the only way to stop it would be to take the column of skin and sinew from which it rose and twist it to silence between my hands.

We will go back to the question of fathers and mothers later, though we must take care not to fall into the swamp of amateur psychoanalysis. Halfway through *The Bell Jar,* nevertheless, we begin to form an idea of what this bell jar is of which Plath writes so frighteningly. It seems it is a kind of vacuum, a vacuum composed of self-canceling values. Some of these values are social and shared with most middle-class Americans; some are domestic and relate to women in society; some are personal and attributable to Esther's ambitions as a writer and her high expectations of herself. Others, of course, have to do with her relationship with her mother and her dead father. But up to the moment of breakdown, all these values have been held together by a bullying will to succeed. When her will weakens, Esther's conflicting self-images collapse in upon each other, leaving a vacuum in which her mind is incapable of breathing. It is because her mind is stifling that she attempts to kill the body that sustains it.

Now, I'd be willing to bet anything that nothing like this ever happened to Emily Dickinson. Miss Dickinson's tortures were religious and personal. She was, to an extreme degree, passionate and shy. Personal relationships were too highly charged for intercourse, so she had to confine her social life to letters. But she accepted the crushing provincial society in which she lived because, as we have seen, it suited the peculiar nature of her genius. Had she been a man she would have had to find a way of life that gave her equal privacy—not easy in nineteenth-century New England, where, if you went into the church, you had to preach to huge congregations, and if you went into literature you were meant to write for the *Atlantic Monthly.* Emerson and Whitman, at periods in their lives, had to work for their bread. Emily Dickinson was spared that indignity. It was no disgrace to be the family spinster. It was luck, and secretly Emily Dickinson knew it. That room with closed doors in the spacious house in

Amherst saw terrible anguish, but it was not the cause of that anguish. It was a refuge from it. This was the principal difference between the bedroom in Amherst and the bedroom in Wellesley.

Other women have known their luck. It is surprising how many spinster writers there have been: Jane Austen, Emily Brontë, Stevie Smith, Charlotte Mew, Marianne Moore, Elizabeth Bishop. These women may have suffered, but they suffered as women who attempted neither to fight male domination nor compromise themselves to suit it. Theirs was a narrow independence, even a selfish one, but it was real. It was bought at the price of what used to be called "womanliness"—sex, marriage, children, and the socially acceptable position of wife.

Sometimes I think a woman writer has to pay that price. In my own case, however, I've not been willing, any more than Sylvia Plath was willing, to sacrifice my life as a woman in order to have a life as a writer. Surely, in the twentieth century, when society allows so much, it ought to be possible to be a fulfilled woman and an independent writer without guilt—or without creating a bell jar vacuum in which it is impossible to breathe. As I look back over my own experience, I see, however, that I have only *just* managed to survive. Writing poetry is not like most jobs; it can't be rushed or done well between household chores—at least not by me. The mood of efficiency, of checking things off the list as you tear through a day's shopping, washing, cleaning, mending, and so forth is totally destructive of the slightly bored melancholy that nurtures imagination. Even friends distract, though I often make them an excuse not to write. It is possible that marriage, children, social obligations have always been ways for me of avoiding the hard work of making poems. But even if this were so, I can't now reverse my decision to have a family. I have to be a writer with a handicap.

One way out of the dilemma of the woman/writer is to write poems about the dilemma itself. Though I have never considered myself to be a specifically feminist poet, many of my poems are about being trapped in domestic surroundings. I dread, and have always dreaded, that marriage, a home, and family would sap my creative energies, that they would devour my time and my personality, that they would, in a venomous way I can't easily explain, use me up. When I look at my early poems I am surprised that so many of them express what seems to me this particularly feminine dread.

The first poem I published in a magazine—when I was about twenty-three—was called "The Women." It was written in Yorkshire in 1956 when, although I didn't know it, I was going through a bell jar experience of my own. I was married to a young Englishman whom I assumed I adored. He was an athlete, a businessman who spent part of his time in the Territorial Army. Obviously his activities in these respects were not ones I could share. He and his friends, mostly just out of Cambridge, were the first men I had met who made me feel that being a girl made any difference to the way you were treated. In my coeducational American university women were, if anything, rather more in control of things than men. My poem, "The Women," however, referred not to the au pair girls and debutantes our life in London perplexed me by including but to the wives of the officers in my husband's regiment.

We were "billeted," I remember, with the colonel and his wife. During the day the men went out on maneuvers; if it was a weekend, they went shooting on the moors. The women stayed at home by the fire, surrounded by vases gorged with dahlias, gossiping, sighing, waiting for the men to come back so we could all broach the drinks cupboard. I spent the greater part of the mornings roaming the blustery streets of Halifax in hopes of bumping into the public library, but after lunch I was condemned to interminable cups of tea. One such afternoon I withdrew to my bedroom and wrote this poem.

> Women, waiting for their husbands,
> sit among dahlias all the afternoons,
> while quiet processional seasons
> drift and subside at the doors like dunes,
> and echoes of ocean curl from the flowered wall.
>
> The room is a murmuring shell of nothing at all.
> As the fire dies under the dahlias, shifting embers
> flake from the silence, thundering when they fall,
> and wives who are faithful waken bathed in slumber;
> the loud tide breaks and turns to bring them breath.

At five o'clock it flows about their death,
and then the dahlias, whirling
suddenly to catherine wheels of surf,
spin on their stems until the shallows sing,
and flower pools gleam like lamps on the lifeless tables.

Flung phosphorescence of dahlias tells
the women time. They wait to be,
prepared for the moment of inevitable
good evening when, back from the deep, from the mystery,
the tritons return and the women whirl in their sea.

After the experience of "The Women" I less frequently indulged my childhood fantasy of becoming a heroine out of Jane Austen, and began to wonder what I really wanted to do. Back in London I tried to write a novel, but like Esther Greenwood, I found I had nothing to say. My poems were better, but when I sent them to English magazines they were turned down. I offered myself to the PEN club in Chelsea as a typist, and they let me type some poems for them. But soon they discovered that I was too poor a typist even for their unpaid standards, and they let me go. I began to feel I hadn't got it in me to be a writer. The terrible parlors of "The Women" yawned before me.

When I had a baby, things got not better but worse. I was determined not to let such a natural event disturb my reading program (I was putting myself through James, Hardy, and Proust), but of course it did, even though I invented a way of breast-feeding and reading at the same time, propping my book up on a music stand. The baby was unimpressed. She howled every evening at dinner time, and since my husband disapproved of babies at our candlelit dinners, meals were served to an accompaniment of sobs—my own and the baby's in about equal proportion. I found, after a while, that I couldn't eat without vomiting, and soon I lost so much weight I had to go to hospital.

Shortly after I was released (no doctor could diagnose my ailment) we began moving, first to a village near Norwich, then to Grimsby, then to Belfast, then to New York, then to a Faulkner-like town called Corinth, Mississippi, and finally to Atlanta, Georgia, where we were divorced. All through this period—1957 to 1959—I was in a state of appalling numbness.

My husband was puzzled, since he was having a difficult time establishing himself in his own business and wanted my support. In return he was prepared to provide me with a house, a maid, and time. Why was I not writing the novels and poems I had promised? When I grew more depressed and spent days and nights weeping, he decided he'd had enough. The terms of divorce taxed us both, since there was no third party except my bell jar. We had to concoct a separation on the grounds of mental cruelty—not mine to him, as so often had been the case, but his to me—which seemed, even to my foggy mind, unfair.

I mention these facts not because they are unique but because they are not. Thousands of educated women with small babies who have followed in the wake of an enterprising husband have undergone the same depressions, the same sense of failure, the same collapse into breakdown, if not divorce. Perhaps Emily Dickinson's father knew what he was talking about when he suggested that too many books joggle the mind. But I still wonder how much my depression had to do with my discontent with a woman's role in marriage and how much it had to do with my inability to write in uncongenial circumstances. The questions were distinct, though linked. Any writer has to keep his or her imagination alive, and that means he or she can't happily live a lie or write well in an alien role. On the other hand, it seems to me now that I blamed too much on the marriage and my role as a woman in it. I should have written in spite of everything that seemed against me. I should not have excused myself.

Luckily we are living in the middle of a century that, for all its drawbacks, allows people who have made a mistake in marriage to go back and try again. I returned to the University of Michigan with my daughter, wrote a book of poems, began a critical book and took an M.A. in English. Curiously, though, I have been unable to use the memory of those unhappy years directly in my poems. The reason for this may be the natural desire of human beings to suppress what is unpleasant. But I think there's a more important reason that has to do with the nature of writing itself. Unless you are setting out to write an autobiographical novel, like *The Bell Jar,* or a novel calculated to shock the public with its frankness, like *Fear of Flying,* it is better art to let your memory knit itself into your subconscious and twine around your imagination until you have found a way of transforming experience into fiction. "Facts," wrote Virginia Woolf, "are a very inferior form of fiction."

The facts of my experience, as I have said, were not interesting in themselves. They were familiar. It is because they were so familiar that they gave me an idea for a long poem that later became *Correspondences*. If I had suffered, in my ignorance of myself, from a sense of ignominy and numbness in marriage, other women must have suffered too. I began to think with troubled resentment of my mother. All through my childhood I'd seen her sacrifice herself and her interests for the sake of my father, myself, and my sisters. She had wanted to be a novelist, and we all encouraged her. But, as in my own case, encouragement only made her feel guilty when she was not doing her "duty" toward us. And when she did her "duty"—and sighed afterward—then *we* felt guilty for taking so much of her time. The process of "wifeing" and "mothering" was steeped in guilt. By modeling myself on my mother, I had plunged unwittingly into the same guilt; but in my slow way, like swimming to the surface of water I was drowning in, I began to realize that guilt could also be an *excuse*. If I had really wanted to write I would have done so. So would my mother. Writing for us was, or could be, wishful thinking. There is always time. No amount of housework or baby-tending takes time from writing if you really want to write. Sylvia Plath wrote her great last poems in the early morning before her babies were awake. Wilfred Owen wrote his best poems in the trenches. Sweet are the uses of adversity.

In a burst of self-knowledge that was unsettling at first, I knew I had rigged that divorce—and all the unhappiness that preceded it—in order not to repeat the experience of my mother. After my mother's death from cancer in the early 1960s (when I married again) I was still unable to rid myself of her image—her ghost. Yet I was inexpressibly upset by her death. I felt I had to tell her something, that she had cheated herself and me by dying just as I was about to speak. It was this urgency to resurrect her and at the same time to kill her spirit (remember Virginia Woolf's struggles with the Angel in the House) that made it impossible for me not to write *Correspondences*. It was a book I couldn't avoid.

The first poem I wrote on this theme—the theme of mothers—was called "Generations." Probably it was the seed from which *Correspondences* grew. It was written when I was living in Glasgow with my second husband and two babies, four years after my mother's death. The bell jar threatened again, but this time I was determined to smash it. Even if I had to be cruel to my family; even if I had to leave them.

"Generations" is a bitter poem where "The Women" is distanced and polite. The women in each stanza represent my grandmother, my mother, and myself in that order . . . three degrees of self-sacrifice.

> Know this mother by her three smiles.
> A grey one drawn over her mouth by frail hooks.
> One hurt smile under each eye.
>
> Know this mother by the frames she makes.
> By the silence in which she suffers each child
> to scratch out the aquatints in her mind.
>
> Know this mother by the way she says
> "darling" with her teeth clenched.
> By the fabulous lies she cooks.

With that poem I felt I had made a breakthrough. Shortly afterward, in 1970, we left Glasgow and lived for six months in Cambridge, Massachusetts, where my husband and I both had scholarships. Mine was at the Radcliffe Institute for Independent Women, and I found myself surrounded there by discontented contemporaries. America itself was in a profound state of discontent. The puritan values of honesty, loyalty, piety, and self-sacrifice I'd been taught to respect in my childhood were everywhere being dismissed. Hippies, drug takers, dropouts, and failed intellectuals lined up for food and psychiatric treatment in the streets of Cambridge. Our flat in a racially mixed area was robbed five times; our four-year-old son was attacked by a gang of black children. All that time I was at Radcliffe writing *Correspondences* I was aware of living through a period of acute crisis. Excitement, despair, challenge, unhappiness, and anger infected the New England air. I began to understand why Sylvia Plath and Anne Sexton had gone mad.

And yet I was determined not to. It would have been too easy. All around me the world seemed mad. Lowell and Plath had set a fashion, and for a poet, madness (with blame on society and capitalist materialism) was all but obligatory. Two things saved me. In the first place, I had found an archive of letters from well-known American families in the Schlesinger Library, and reading them, I decided I could use them in a poem. The only way to fight the madness of the present was to gain some understanding of the past. I discovered a trunk of family letters in my sister's basement in New York, and these, too, profoundly moved me. In the second place, we had a weekly escape route from Harvard to Vermont. We drove up to my family's house in Wilmington nearly every weekend, and it was there I decided to set my poem in a mythical Clearfield, and make Vermont and the peace it stood for a symbol of the more solid America that had disappeared from the demented cities. I don't know when it occurred to me that my poem should take the form of letters. I think the family letters themselves suggested it; their language was already poetry, Victorian, distant. Why had no one thought of writing an epistolary poem before?

The central character in *Correspondences* is a woman like my mother—liberal, generous, self-sacrificing, devoted to good causes and prone to idealizing her family. I called her Ruth after Ruth in the Bible, the daughter of Naomi, who, you may remember, calls herself "Mara," meaning bitter. I turned Mara into the woman's name, Maura, and created both Maura and Ruth in the image of the self-sacrificing mother. Maura sacrifices her independent life as a writer to marry an idealistic but impractical reformer. Ruth sacrifices a lover to devote herself to her kindly but unexciting husband. In both cases I suspect these women took the *happiest* course open to them. That is to say, I doubt that Maura in 1900 would ever have become more than a mediocre writer; and Ruth, in 1940, was certainly better off with her unpretentious American. Nonetheless, neither one of these women was willing to take risks, and their happiness was bordered with wistfulness, with a longing for knowledge beyond their experience.

It is Ruth's children who are given the opportunity of risk, and two of them take it. Kay marries a fashionable psychiatrist in New York, has a baby, becomes very unhappy, and leaves her husband after a nervous breakdown. Nick, her younger brother, leaves New England after his mother's funeral and heads west, deserting his career at college. Only Eden, Kay's younger sister, stays at home in Vermont, trying to preserve the family's values.

The title, *Correspondences,* refers partly to the letters of the two sisters, Eden and Kay, each of whom confronts a disintegrating world that, after their mother's death, is impossible to hold together. Eden, in Vermont, discovers a box of family letters, dating from the 1830s, and in part 1 these letters make up the *Correspondences* within the correspondence of the sisters. Part 2 is entitled "Women in Marriage" and concerns three generations of women, Maura, Ruth, and Kay—the grandmother, mother, and daughter of "Generations." Each of these women makes a different compromise in her marriage. Part 3 is composed of journals written by Ruth's husband, Neil Arbeiter, and her son Nick. The entire poem ends with a letter from Kay to her father in which she explains her reasons for not being able to return to New England from London, to which she has made a partially satisfactory escape.

> "In the floodtides of *Civitas Mundi*
> New England is dissolving like a green chemical.
> Old England bleeds out to meet it in mid-ocean.
>   Nowhere is safe."
>
> It is a poem I can't continue.
> It is America I can't contain.
>
> Dear Father, I love but can't know you.
>   I've given you all that I can.
>   Can these pages make amends for what was not said?
>   Do justice to the living, to the dead?

You can see, even from the little I've said, that *Correspondences* is about more than women's predicament in American history. It was intended to be a study of puritan values in New England— of their strengths, their weaknesses, their corruption by ambition and greed, and their final overthrow in the world of Vietnam and Watergate. Yet, as I wrote I could not help but be aware of the amount of my own experience that was going into it. In each generation there is misunderstanding between the women and the men. In 1830, for instance, Elizabeth Boyd is all but crushed by her Calvinist father for not accepting the judgment of God when her husband is drowned. In 1840, Marianne Chandler, who loves parties but hates sex, suffers from the sexual blundering of her puritanical husband. Later he divorces her with contemptuous blame.

> Of the causes of strife between us—
> your selfishness, your vanity, your whims, wife,
> your insistent and querulous disobedience,
> no more.
> It is enough for you to live with your naked conscience
> upon which must lie the death of our infant daughter
> as her innocent body lies, unfulfilled in its grave.
> Farewell.
> Find peace if you can with your sister,
> her friends and fashions.
> Frivolity is an armor of lace
> against the mind's inner vengeance and poisons.

In later generations of Chandlers, pompous Jacob tells his daughter off for wasting her time "scribbling" in college when she should be taking care of her mother at home.

> Maura! Maura! Those kisses were never gifts.
> Bestowed as they were with the charity of Our Lord Himself,
> those kisses were loans! Loans upon interest these many
> long years! Now it is time to repay them graciously,
> selflessly, with little acts of kindness and understanding.

In 1900, Maura, chastened at last, determines to give up her dream of becoming a writer and vows to devote her life to her impractical, idealist husband, Ethan Boyd.

> What does Nature
> ask of Woman?
> Give to him that needeth.
> Employ the hour that passeth.
> Be resolute in submission.
> Love thy husband.
> Bear children.

Ruth, Maura's daughter, tries to follow in her mother's footsteps, but falls in love with an English novelist—a plummy, selfish fellow whose pseudosophistication impresses her. She lives a secret, divided life with her husband until she dies of cancer, publicly virtuous but privately horrified and undermined by a devouring sense of guilt. In a letter to her lover in 1945, she writes of this guilt.

> And what are these terrible things
> they are taking for granted? Air and grass,
> houses and beds, laundry and things to eat—
> so little clarity, so little space between them;
> a crowd of distractions to be
> bought and done and arranged for,
> drugs for the surely incurable pain of
> living misunderstood among many who love you.

Finally, for Kay, Ruth's daughter, the fiber of a repressive society breaks down just as she herself does. In 1954 she finds she can no longer tolerate her life in Westchester County and runs away to New York. But in an asylum she discovers there is no escape in madness either. Having rejected her mother, Kay at last turns to her for help. And yet she knows there is no way back to her mother's beliefs; any compromise with a former life will be forced. The hysteria at the end of this poem is one many of us felt in the 1950s and 1960s; Sylvia Plath was spokeswoman for a whole generation of Kays.

> Come when you can, or when
> the whitecoats let you.
> But they may not let you, of course.
> They think you're to blame.
> Good God, mother, I'm not insane!
> How can I get out of here?
> Can't you get me out of here?
>
> I'll try, I'll try, really,
> I'll try again. The marriage.
> The baby. The house. The whole damn bore!
>
> Because for me, what the hell else is there?
> Mother, what more? What more?

Naturally, when I was writing that poem I realized Kay was a version of myself. All that I had suffered in my first marriage, all that I had felt about my child, my husband, my mother, came together in it. It was a poem I found painful to write. And yet, Kay is not me, either. She is a sort of Esther Greenwood. I have never had a breakdown in a museum or lived in Westchester County or been married to a fashionable psychiatrist. Kay's *feelings,* her mixed love and hatred for her child, her sense of imprisonment in her house, her impulse to fly, to escape to drink or to an anonymous city—these feelings *have* been mine. They can be found in other poems . . . in one called "In the House," for instance, which I wrote long before any of the poems of *Correspondences.*

> Whatever it is, it's clear it has claims on me.
> Its surface establishes itself
> outside and around me,
> drawing me through or into
> what I take to be my proper dominion.
>
> These keys are my keys, this door my door.
> The interior is entirely familiar . . .
>
> Again, these interminable stairs, bristling with children.
> "Mother, mother," they wail. They bleat with desire.
> They quarrel and hold up their wounds to be kissed.
> And yet when I bend to them
> It's like kissing a photograph.
> I taste chemicals.
> My lips meet unexpectedly a flatness.

But in Kay's poem from *Correspondences* I learned how to put experience into poetry without "confessing" it. I should add, too, that the "facts" pertaining to the Chandler family in my poem differ from those pertaining to my own family history. The nearer I came to my time and to people I knew, the more imperative it seemed to me to get feelings right but to invent "facts." Apart from the embarrassment of taking family skeletons out of cupboards before the flesh is off, so to speak, fiction has to be more obvious than life. A reader has to see reasons for feelings in behavior.

But I see I have left the subject of women and women writers and got on to a theory of literature. I still haven't answered the question I asked at the beginning of this essay. Is it possible for a woman to be an adult, married, sexual person and a poet as well?

In one sense, poems like those I have quoted answer the question by writing about it. If—as women—our theme is woman's survival and self-discovery, then we have found a subject that meets the requirements of experience both as women and as writers. In the 1970s, too, we can say what we please. We no longer need to be embarrassed by social taboos. The problem, however, does not really concern itself with sexual explicitness. For a woman it goes deeper. I encountered it when I had finished *Correspondences,* for I realized then that I had written a woman's book—that is to say, the experiences of my characters were experiences I understood through having lived my life as a woman. The two world wars are scarcely mentioned. The Civil War is recognized only as it divides the family into allegiances North and South. Now, there are many people these days who would say that women's books are just what women should be writing. The American poet, Adrienne Rich, for example, believes that women are awakening into a shared, powerful consciousness of what it means to be female. The "drive to self-knowledge," she says, "is more than a search for identity; it is part of her refusal of the self-destructiveness of male-dominated society." We must find, she thinks, a language of our own to express "a whole new psychic geography" of female emotion.

For my part, despite *Correspondences,* I am inclined to disagree with Adrienne Rich. I am not convinced that women need a specifically female language to describe female experience. The question of language is in any case an especially thorny one. For even if we agree that women have a less aggressive, more instinctive, more "creative" nature than men (and I'm not sure that's true) language is difficult to divide into sexes. A good writer's imagination should be bisexual or transsexual. The only society I know of in which men and women traditionally have spoken different languages—and accepted roles accordingly—developed in Japan. At the risk of digression, let me remind you that in tenth-century Japan women wrote poetry and fiction in the vernacular (the language of society, love, grace, beauty), while men did business, politics and went about extending their territorial rights in Classical Chinese. The result of this sexual differentiation in language was a vast and marvelous literature created almost exclusively by women (high-class, aristocratic women, mind you) of which Lady Murasaki's *Tale of Genji* is perhaps the most famous example.

A flight of fancy prompts me to imagine a woman's language that appoints itself guardian of the traditional beauties of English as opposed to the speed-read efficiencies of American. Imagine a woman's language that preserves the dignity of the *King James Bible* and the *Prayer Book,* which forbids the use of technological jargon in any work of literature not intended for the laboratory or classroom. But such a dream is, of course, impossible. In our democratic society, such an exclusive language would be hooted down as "irrelevant"—not least by women who ask for equality at the same time as asking for an independent consciousness and a language of their own in which to express it.

For better or worse, women and men writers in the West, in the later twentieth century, share a common consciousness. Their language is a reflection, or even a definition, of that consciousness. If anything we want *more* communication, *more* understanding between the sexes. We are beginning to see that though our physical functions differ (necessarily) our psychic needs are alike. If there is to be a new creative consciousness— one that is not based on phallic values of conquest, power, ambition, greed, murder, and so forth—then this consciousness must have room for both male and female; a consciousness the greatest literature has, in fact, been defining for a long time.

What has all this to do with *Correspondences* and the writing of women's books? Well, now that *Correspondences* has been written, I'm proud of it. Through it I crossed a bridge—or rather built a bridge—into the twentieth century. All the anger, the confusion, the misery, and the doubt I experienced during the 1950s and 1960s went into it, and because they were a woman's angers and miseries, they exposed part of the general consciousness of the age—a part that in the past had been suppressed.

But now I want to stand on the shoulders of *Correspondences,* as it were, and look at a wider world. For both sexes it is important that we understand each other and the world we have to share. There must be no suppression and no playacting either. For me it is as fraudulent to adopt the role of a "new" woman as that of an "old" one; being a writer proscribes role-playing. In both cases the role that is offered substitutes a public stance for particular perceptions. And a writer must leave herself free for particular perceptions.

Of course, choosing what often feels like a selfish independence means that one pays a price—a high price—in human terms. I don't think you can write truthfully and be entirely comfortable. Tension is a mainspring of the imagination. And something has to be sacrificed—the satisfaction of a role, the satisfaction of a cause, the satisfaction, even, of a sense of guilt. This is why I should like to conclude with a poem I wrote last year called "The Price." What I hoped to imply in this poem is that a price is asked for every engagement with the truth—but it need not be a price that destroys affection. It is also the price *of* affection, since what is most valuable in human understanding is so often what is least definable as politics or even as right or wrong.

> The fear of loneliness, the wish
> to be alone;
> love grown rank as seeding grass
> in every room,
> and anger at it, raging at it
> storming it down.
>
> Also that four-walled chrysalis
> and impediment, home;
> that lamp and hearth, that easy fit
> of bed to bone;
> those children, too, sharp witnesses
> of all I've done.
>
> My dear, the ropes that bind us
> are safe to hold;
> the walls that crush us keep us
> from the cold.
> I know the price and still I pay it, pay it—
> words, their furtive kiss,
> illicit gold.

Some Observations on Women and Tradition

A Letter to Sharon Bryan

You have asked me to comment on my feelings about what you see as a predominantly male tradition in English/American literature. Citing a passage from T. S. Eliot's essay "Tradition and the Individual Talent," you specifically ask if, as a woman writer, I feel left out. My answer is no. The question appears to me to lie quite outside the issues Eliot addressed in that essay. Although everyone knows that women have had a tough time finding acceptance in almost all other professions and fields of study, it seems to me difficult to prove that in Britain and America over the past two hundred years women have not held their own as writers, particularly as writers of fiction. To that I will come later. But first, suppose we look closely at Eliot's essay and the terms it employs.

Tradition, as used in literary criticism, appears to be a word that emerged late, under pressure of modern usage. Eliot himself introduced it in the 1920s out of a new and heightened consciousness of poetry's historical lineage. The essay in question begins cautiously. "In English writing we seldom speak of tradition, though we occasionally apply its name in deploring its absence." He seems to be identifying a point of view, a state of affairs that may not objectively exist. "Seldom, perhaps," he goes on, "does the word appear except in a phrase of censure." The *Oxford English Dictionary* offers no examples of literary tradition. An old word derived from the Latin *traditio,* it apparently has ecclesiastical roots, denoting the transmission or handing down of the rules and ceremonies of the church. A further definition gives "the action of transmitting . . . from one to another, or from generation to generation . . . beliefs, rules, customs, or the like, esp. by word of mouth or *by practice without writing*" (my italics).

From *Where We Stand: Women Poets on Literary Tradition,* ed. Sharon Bryan (New York and London: W. W. Norton and Co., 1993). Reprinted with permission.

Tradition, in a traditional sense, then, would seem to apply chiefly to custom. It may be a term that does not ask to be made explicit until it provokes opposition. When a style of writing incontrovertibly belongs to a period—as Shakespeare's conceits are "Elizabethan" and Jane Austen's prose is "Johnsonian"—the question of tradition does not arise. Only in times of uncertainty, when custom no longer asserts a previously unchallenged authority, is it called upon to play a persuasive role in arguments concerning values. The notion of rebelling against a norm by *defying* tradition can be traced back to the English Reformation's reaction against the Catholic Church. Milton coupled the word with the equally frowned upon *superstition* in *Paradise Lost:* "and the truth / With superstitions and traditions taint" (XII, 512).

In the first quarter of the present century—a time of social transformation and uncertainty comparable to Milton's—Eliot, with the backing of F. R. Leavis, found the concept of a tradition indispensable to his modernist polemic. It is easier to understand now than when Eliot was writing why "Tradition and the Individual Talent" had to be constructed primarily as a bastion of defense. After the First World War, Eliot (rightly) anticipated the disintegration of an aesthetic inheritance he held to be particularly precious. His personal desire to salvage what he called "the historical sense" led him to define tradition in such a way as to preserve what he saw as valuable in the past while giving himself full license to forge ahead with literary experiment. Today it appears that this essay by a poet famous for his insistence on the impersonality of the artist can be read as an intensely personal plea. At its heart is a statement of the central time-motif in Eliot's major work:

> the historical sense involves a perception, not only of the pastness of the past, but of its presence; the historical sense compels a man to write not merely with his own generation in his bones, but with a feeling that the whole of the literature of Europe . . . has a simultaneous existence and composes a simultaneous order. This historical sense, which is a sense of the timeless as well as of the temporal and of the timeless and of the temporal together, is what makes a writer traditional. And it is at the same time what makes a writer most acutely conscious of his place in time, of his contemporaneity.

Whatever you make of "time present and time past . . . both perhaps present in time future," it must be allowed that the exclusion of women had no part in the poet's purpose. It would never have crossed Eliot's mind that a body of feminists in the late years of this extraordinary century might take offense. Nor would he have considered the fourteenth-century anchoress Julian of Norwich, quoted in the third part of "Little Gidding," to be in any way isolated from the tradition because she was a woman mystic. Surely, the plane on which Eliot conceived of poetry, like it or not, had nothing to do with today's political scuffling between the sexes; and if women writers feel excluded from what they read into his meaning, it seems to me that they are misjudging a *literary* essay written by a particular man in particular circumstances, in order to make out, in quite different circumstances, a *political* case for initiating a tradition of their own.

Many people would argue, these days, that there is no literature that is not subliminally political; and Eliot, too, was aware of the political dimensions of his "historical sense," that is, that literary imagination is often responsible for the selective discriminations of history. I would question, however, the legitimacy of searching through Eliot's texts like self-appointed members of a thought-police for proof that "patriarchy" lay at the root of his criticism; that his use of the masculine noun and possessive pronoun "man"/"his" betrays his "masculinism"; that his whole mode of discourse disregards woman's just cause for resentment after ages of cultural exclusion. By now critics too easily reach for the equalizing terminology of postmodernism; and we also hear—thanks to a somewhat surprising injection of Freud into feminist theory—a great deal about subliminal discrimination and the unconscious prejudice of language. To me, such arguments only offer more examples of a lamentable fin de siècle tendency to bundle up social and psychological perceptions into ideological sandbags and then employ them in argument as if they were the building blocks of some ultimate social (and of course prescriptively moral) enlightenment.

Poor old Eliot, poor old Dr. Leavis. The literary values that these sometimes misguided but basically humane men sought to establish—aesthetic, moral, and historical but not in any way designed to promote one gender at the expense of the other (Leavis championed two women novelists out of four in his *Great Tradition*)—have been smashed to smithereens in less than fifty years of bullying political ideology. To be sure, if we choose to consider men as a class of beings distinct from and opposed to women (and I don't think we ought to), then we also have to grant that one sex alone has brought Western culture to its present state of crisis and intellectual overkill. Perhaps it has not been altogether a bad thing that women have had to employ themselves more practically. We women should be all the better prepared to puncture male afflatus with little pins of skepticism. How much academic clout and subsidized importance the theorizing men of the late twentieth century have attracted to themselves, with their dangerous isms and ologies! How much dictatorial power in the field of literature they have wielded! How many trees have been sacrificed to bring out their thousands of unreadable books!

And women academics, meanwhile? How have feminist critics, as a body, responded over the past forty years to this intimidating, jargon-studded blitz? Instead of splitting their sides with laughter, or, more to the point, polishing the art of exact perception and drawing on the wit, wisdom, sensibility, and deep suspicion of power they inherit from the female side of the English literary tree, they have hurried around in a panic looking for ways to adapt the jargon of these overserious and ridiculously pompous men to their own sectarian and mainly self-justifying purposes.

What a situation! As if literary criticism were a more impressive and admirable profession than the writing of literature at first hand. How much easier, how much grander, how much more lucrative it is to establish a system of categories and caveats than to incur the aesthetic and financial risks of writing poetry or fiction oneself. No wonder some critics have done their best to abolish the concept of the author. The idea that the "culture" is responsible for producing a poem or a novel makes it possible for a critic, in the name of that abstract concept, to claim credit as a cocreator.

This is not to argue that literary criticism is worthless. The response and considered opinion of an informed scholar who honestly and passionately elucidates a text can be of untold value—everybody knows that. And, yes, there are some fine women critics about. Writers themselves usually make the best critics because, even when wrong, they care so much about writing well. Why, one wonders, do not more women novelists and poets take on criticism? Is it because they don't want to risk polluting their creative sensibilities, or is it that some of them still hide behind the old-fashioned idea that women, being born intuitive, write while men, being born logical, think? If the latter, then vigorous writer-thinkers like Adrienne Rich mistakenly make a case for a self-enclosed, self-protective feminist language of feelings. A more liberal approach would be to admit that some imaginative writers, both men and women, enjoy thinking abstractly and grow through doing so; others find critical writing unnourishing or destructive of their gifts. Where is your reason for a gender-specific tradition in either case?

Young American women of my generation (I graduated from the University of Michigan in 1954) listened to Eliot, Leavis, and the fathers of the New Criticism because they taught us not only *what* was important to read, but *how* to read; how, that is, to pay close attention to words, how to look for what was fresh or stale, convincing or weak in the literature we studied. It's that *how* that stays with me as the most valuable lesson of my college years, and not the *who* or *what* of anyone's prescriptive theory. I still believe that the re-readability of a book—long after its time— secures it a place in tradition, and not the gender of its author.

Given such a perspective, you can see why, in my view, it matters hardly at all whether the books history has shown to be re-readable—loved over many generations—were written by men or by women. I don't say differences don't exist. No reader could fail to see, say, that Fielding's full-blooded social range was not available to Jane Austen. Who, though, was the finer writer? As the nineteenth century wore on, women's writing engaged, like men's, with a larger social spectrum. As for our own permissive time, women certainly have as much access to public wickedness and folly as men. As human beings, we are all flawed, wrong, sorry, tragic and comic, guided and influenced by each other, subject to the temptations of vanity, worldliness, and all the assorted ills of nature. That is the human condition "traditional" writing engages with, and it shines in a recognizable form through all literature worth reading.

Writers like Virginia Woolf, contemporary with Eliot and incensed at their exclusion from what they increasingly perceived to be a man's world—and botched at that—quite rightly made a fuss about being confined to the parlor, bedroom, and kitchen. All honor to them. Today the male establishment is being persuaded into accepting the justice of sharing with women responsibility for public life. The question that arises is whether women, especially imaginative women, are going to like it. For anyone who finds writing a demanding, difficult art, it is generally an advantage to be free of institutional pressures and absolved from the necessity of making a living.

When I began to write I believed that taking a job in publishing or teaching would stimulate me to produce. I soon found I had no energy for literature after a day's work, especially as I had to attend to my family when I came home. How fortunate Stevie Smith had been, I thought, in her suburban seclusion. Virginia Woolf, socially privileged and without children, hadn't known the half of what family stress could be. No wonder most women writers in the past had decided (or had the decision thrust upon them) not to marry. Thanks to contraception and an independence that would have amazed and deeply shocked our ancestors, women today are encouraged to advance their careers in two or three directions at once, but does that make them any better poets or artists?

When I look around me at the disasters of contemporary education in our market-fixated, viciously competitive culture, I'm tempted to argue that, given reasonable encouragement, women writers today—as individuals—are neither better nor worse off than they were a hundred years ago. Perhaps it was easier then. No one intimated to Mrs. Gaskell or Mrs. Humphrey Ward that they ought to keep a lookout for the dimensions of a women's collective psyche. Being unencumbered by theory, they wrote, one assumes, because they had something to say and were good at it. Or because writing brought them money, friends, and fame. Some women poets were eccentric—but then so were men poets. Nineteenth-century society may have ignored spinster daughters, turned its back on genius, and taken inferior authors to heart, but that is no more than happens today. Some social injustices we castigate from the perspective of the 1990s are likely to be exaggerated by our predisposition to see all women artists up to and including Sylvia Plath as victims of a patriarchal system. I can't believe, though, that ambitious women in nineteenth-century England, even if they were educated at home, were more discriminated against than gifted men of the working classes such as William Blake and John Clare.

Most writers today would agree that in a fair society, what goes for men ought to go for women; opportunities and freedoms taken for granted by privileged groups ought to be offered to the less fortunate. Yes, of course. Yet the underside of the democratic process is that competition among a large number of people tends to favor those who best please the dogma makers of their day. And poets, of whatever sex, have always felt a strong need to break cultural rules. They may make better citizens if they double as teachers of creative writing or spend time organizing festivals and editing partisan anthologies, but it's a rare poet who manages to fulfill a particular group's expectations and remain a force for the future. For poetry *is* a personal "process," Eliot's word again; and the best writers of whatever sex, race, or political persuasion have to give themselves over to it in the face of constant failure and frustration.

The woman poets I favor, though feminists, have not put writing poetry at the service of their politics. What a self-perpetuating critical establishment, male or female, approves of or not is fundamentally of no concern to them. For when a poet or novelist is "really writing," as Sylvia Plath put it—slipping perhaps into sudden ease after a long struggle with the extraneous—then the whole labeling apparatus of criticism, ideology, competition, and self-consciousness becomes irrelevant.

The Biographer as Fiction Maker
Writing on Sylvia Plath

In the autumn of 1989, Viking (Penguin) in London and Houghton Mifflin in Boston published *Bitter Fame*, the biography of Sylvia Plath I had written, in a lurid atmosphere of distorting judgments and intensifying passions, at the invitation of Plath's sister-in-law, Olwyn Hughes. Before I began *Bitter Fame* I had drafted a short "guide" to Plath for a series Penguin Books was bringing out at the time. After reading my draft, Ted Hughes sent me a long typed letter in which he partly explained why he had kept silent over the years. His chief concern had been to give his and Plath's young children as far as possible a normal childhood. Although he and Sylvia Plath had been estranged at the time of her death, they were not legally separated; he had half expected a reconciliation. Instead, she killed herself. The devastated Hughes returned to his Devon home solely responsible for Frieda (age three) and Nicholas (still a baby). He adopted a policy of fending off intrusive journalists, biographers, hagiographers, and self-appointed detectives. With time and silence the wound would heal.

As it happened, radical attacks on Hughes, amplified by uninformed representations of his first marriage, never ceased to plague him. His children were permitted to grow up in peace, but the wound Hughes himself sustained had never been allowed to heal. The scab that should have been forming over it had been picked off so many times that the injury had become a permanent infection. In the poetry Ted Hughes had written up to that time, he had rigorously eschewed the mode of personal confession that Robert Lowell and his followers were practicing in America. Nor did Hughes seek to justify himself in the one contribution he allowed himself to make to the writing of *Bitter*

This chapter has its origins in a lecture on the writing of *Bitter Fame, A Life of Sylvia Plath*, given in Hebden Bridge, Yorkshire on September 28, 1993, and revised for the Kings Lynn Festival of Literature, May 1994. It was further revised in 1997.

Fame. An image that remains with me from his letter is that of a boy with a fox in his arms, trying to protect it from pursuing hounds, the fox biting him the while. Before I even discussed with Olwyn Hughes the possible expansion of my guide into a full-length biography, I was sure that "the Hugheses' side" of the story needed to be told.

That my own relations with the Plath estate were fraught during the writing of *Bitter Fame* I shall not attempt to conceal, but from a distance of nearly ten years it is easier now than it was then to see why I ran into difficulties. Wounded and numbed by events that must damn him in the eyes of the world (Assia Wevill followed the example of Plath and destroyed herself and her child in 1969), he was entrusted with the selecting and editing of Plath's unpublished work. This he did with great sensitivity, showing himself over the years to be one of Plath's wisest and most understanding critics. He took advice before adding Plath's last, desperate lyrics to the manuscript of *Ariel,* knowing how he would be pilloried had he left these wonderful poems out. He was excoriated for disregarding the poet's plan to end the book with the bee sequence. Not wanting his children ever to read what Hughes considered to be the insane accusations of Plath's final journal, he burned it. That quite understandable action gave his enemies real grounds for charging him with self-interested censorship. Under renewed fire from feminists, many of them American, he passed the day-to-day management of Plath's estate to his sister Olwyn, who had recently set up as a literary agent. Olwyn, like her brother, was fiercely protective of her family's privacy. Both were particularly concerned to protect Plath's mother from the painful knowledge of how much her daughter had written that would hurt her.

When I undertook to write *Bitter Fame* early in 1986, two would-be biographers had already broken down under the strain. In the 1980s a feminist academic, Linda Wagner-Martin, was tougher minded, but she ran into a brick wall when she refused to take into account the lengthy, condemning testimony of Dido Merwin. Merwin had witnessed at first hand the breakdown of the Hugheses' marriage and blamed it squarely on Plath. Olwyn Hughes backed Merwin, and in the end Wagner-Martin was denied permission to quote from copyright material.

By the time I came on the scene, Olwyn Hughes was being accused by many in the escalating Plath industry of wickedly trying to suppress "the truth" in order to shield her brother. She was looking for a biographer who, without denying the power and importance of Plath's poetry, would nevertheless listen to Dido Merwin's and her own accounts of what they saw as Plath's unpredictable, spectacularly manipulative behavior.

As for me, I believed then that any worthwhile biography of Plath must focus on her poetry. I had drafted my Penguin guide on the basis of her writings. The poems, the letters, and the journals provided evidence enough of the contradictory dreams and imaginings that had created Plath, the poet. Anything that outside witnesses could add to the poet's self-portrait would be fascinating but essentially extraneous. If I had persisted with my original book I would have produced a careful reading of the poems set within a rough sketch of the life. The book would have stirred up no controversy whatsoever.

Olwyn, however, argued that a biography is by definition *the story of a life,* and the impressions that Plath's life had made on other people must feature in its telling. Grasping that I was unused to gathering information from "witnesses" and had no taste for literary detective work, she decided to help me. She introduced me to Dido Merwin and persuaded Merwin to let me have copies of the letters she had written to Linda Wagner-Martin. She then got in touch with some of Ted Hughes's friends who had known Plath and persuaded them to break the silence Hughes had hitherto insisted upon. She arranged for me to meet Lucas Myers, who had seen much of Plath at Cambridge, and to correspond with the Irish poet Richard Murphy. With myself and Judith Flanders, a brilliant young editor at Penguin, she hosted a lunch meeting with Jillian Becker, in whose house the poet had spent her last days. It was Olwyn's wish to include the reminiscences of Lucas Myers, Dido Merwin, and Richard Murphy as appendices to *Bitter Fame.* (Excepting Dido Merwin's acid memoir, these are not unsympathetic to Plath.) Both Jillian Becker and Plath's doctor, when they spoke to me privately, demonstrated how helpless even the most concerned or professional observer can feel when confronted with a person in the process of mental disintegration. By the time I flew to America to consult the archives in the

Lilly Library in Indiana, I felt I understood pretty well why Olwyn Hughes wanted "the Hugheses' side of the story" to be made public.

Passing through New England, I spent a few days consulting Houghton Mifflin's editor Peter Davison, who had known Plath before she went to England. Neither Davison nor Plath's former roommate at Smith, with whom I also spoke, gave me grounds for doubting that the poet's wonderful achievements had come at a terrible cost. The energy she devoted to making herself into a major poet was rarely strong enough to protect her from the anguish she experienced as a person. I saw no reason to disbelieve the gist of what Olwyn, Dido, or Peter Davison had told me when, in the library at Indiana, I found myself strongly sympathizing with Plath. Her papers and letters did confirm that she was at times "terribly upset." There was surely a crack or schism in her personality that she was struggling to heal through her art. The mythos behind her poems was not unconsciously arrived at; on the contrary, with Ted Hughes's help (as Plath's journals and letters repeatedly insist) she had taught herself to draw almost flawless poetry from the deepest, most distraught levels of her mind.

I got back to England with a much clearer idea of the book I wanted to write. Unhappily, I was prevented from getting on with it by an outraged Olwyn Hughes, who had expected I would go on working in tandem with her, and by two passionately concerned women, former friends of Plath (not Hughes), who had been alerted to the influence Olwyn was having over my manuscript. Clarissa Roche and Elizabeth Sigmund were on the telephone to me soon after I had returned to London, and at first I was pleased to hear from them a version of Sylvia Plath that confirmed not *their* views, but *mine*. For by now I was sure Plath had acted different roles with different people (which, though she was a special case, is no more than most of us do) and had found *only in her writing* a means of reconciling her clashing selves and desires.

Olwyn Hughes and I agreed, really, about the psychological genesis of Plath's poems, but Olwyn insisted that my book should show in detail how Plath's "bad behavior," and not Hughes's, had ruined their marriage. Sigmund and Roche, who found a strange ally in Plath's London neighbor Trevor Thomas, were equally sure that Plath was a victim of Ted's unfaithfulness and neglect. The two sides were at the time irreconcilable; as far as I know, they still are. Meanwhile, I was trying to tell the story of an ambitious, gifted American woman who, after marrying the one man in the world who could help her write her poems, drove him out of her life when she discovered he had been unfaithful, and later, though her two tiny children were asleep in the house, gassed herself in her London kitchen. Either *everybody* who had known Plath should be encouraged to give testimony, or *no one* should. I began to think that my first instinct in undertaking a book on Sylvia Plath had been right: concentrate on the work and let the life take care of itself. But by the time I had come back to this conclusion it was too late. The biography was all but complete. Much of it seemed to me and to Peter Davison, who was patiently smoothing out Olwyn's and my disagreements, fair and valuable. Writing the final draft of *Bitter Fame* was a nightmare that I have no intention of reliving in memory. In the aftermath of publication, I defended a biography I had tried to make sympathetic and unbiased. I gave talks here and there, explaining and complaining by turn, but it was not until I met Janet Malcolm that I realized the extent to which I had been persuaded to take on an impossible job. Janet Malcolm's biography of Sylvia Plath's biographers, *The Silent Woman,* was published in the *New Yorker* in August 1993, appearing in book form early in 1994. It is a cogent example of a new postmodernist genre and defines a new kind of biographer's game altogether.

Taking for her subject Sylvia Plath and the feuds that since her death have plagued readers of her poetry, Malcolm managed to direct public interest away from the poet's suicide to the more pertinent issue of how biography does or does not relate to "the truth." Even before embarking on *The Silent Woman,* Malcolm went out of her way to annoy her journalistic confreres by casting doubt on the ethics of their and her profession. "Every journalist who is not too stupid or too full of himself to notice what is going on knows that what he does is morally indefensible," she wrote notoriously in *The Journalist and the Murderer* (1990), attacking the journalist Joe McGinniss for ensnaring the trust of a convicted murderer and then exposing him mercilessly in a book that purported to defend him. Malcolm went on, "He [the journalist] is a kind of confidence man, preying on people's vanity, ignorance or loneliness, gaining their trust and then betraying them without remorse."

Similarly in *The Silent Woman*, Malcolm throws doubt on biography's moral brief, likening a biographer to "the professional burglar" who breaks into a house, rifles through private drawers, and bears valuable loot away before the helpless victim realizes what he has given up. It has not escaped Janet Malcolm's reviewers that in writing a book herself out of interviews with Plath's friends and biographers she was practicing the profession she condemns. Well, so she was; I believe it was her intention to do just that. By reenacting the crime, by throwing herself straight into the biographical predicament, muck and all, she emerged smirched (as she knew she would) yet bearing away a number of insights that biographers sometimes prefer to look away from. One of these is that objectivity on the part of both interviewer and interviewee in a biographical encounter is virtually unattainable. Acts of speaking or writing about human events—especially those we care about—are always to a greater or lesser extent subjectively swayed. We reveal not facts but interpretations.

Another of Malcolm's conclusions is that a biographer who is aware of his or her impudence, who is sensitive to witnesses' feelings and fights shy of invading other people's privacy, will probably never produce a popular piece of work. Of *Bitter Fame,* Malcolm writes, "Every now and then, a biography comes along that strangely displeases the public. Something causes the reader to back away from the writer and refuse to accompany him down the corridor. What the reader has usually heard in the text—what has alerted him to danger—is the sound of doubt, the sound of a crack opening in the wall of the biographer's self-assurance. As a burglar should not pause to discuss with his accomplice the rights and wrongs of burglary while he is jimmying a lock, so a biographer ought not to introduce doubts about the legitimacy of the biographical enterprise. The biography-loving public does not want to hear that biography is a flawed genre. It prefers to believe that certain biographers are bad guys."

Janet Malcolm exaggerates a little when she declares that *Bitter Fame,* once published, was "brutally attacked" and myself "pilloried." Several long, well-considered reviews appeared, both in English and American periodicals. On balance, though, the journalistic response was hostile—quite nasty enough to plunge me into a state of mind not unlike Ted Hughes's. When Janet Malcolm phoned and asked to interview me, I thought she was asking intelligent questions. She perceived that I was depressed, frustrated by not being able to justify my book without seeming to be a feeble tool. Reviewers who made it their business to harry Olwyn Hughes accused me of being clay in her hands. Others who had made reputations out of their versions of Plath's suicide were pleased to believe that I was jealous and therefore easily bribed into producing a pro-Hughes story. Olwyn Hughes, very much hurt, regarded me not only as an incompetent who had never understood the nature of the biographer's brief, but much more unfavorably, as a traitor who, while pretending to listen to her, had all the time been dealing with the enemy behind her back. No wonder I welcomed a sympathetic ear. Janet Malcolm and I had been contemporaries at the University of Michigan. We had even worked in the same room in the Students Publications Building; Malcolm had been an editor of the *Gargoyle* while I was on the staff of the arts magazine, *Generation*. I talked to her in 1992 as to an old friend. I thought I had nothing to lose and quite a lot to gain by being candid.

Later, when *The Silent Woman* appeared in the *New Yorker* I was cross with myself, not Malcolm, for allowing my wounded feelings to dominate our interviews. Like any other naïve interviewee, I had given away far more of myself than I had intended. How could I have been so foolish? Why had I shown myself to be pitiful and weak when, in fact, the entire experience of writing *Bitter Fame* had given me plenty to think about and even a kind of strength. I noted, for example, that almost everyone who had known Plath had a story to tell about him- or herself. Some had views they thought I should express for them; others were eager to play a small part in a large drama. Several were capable of honest detachment, yet even when these most trustworthy witnesses went out of their way to be fair and disinterested, they had to look back over thirty years to a pattern of events they could not possibly remember without the intervening knowledge of what had happened at the end. If it's all but impossible to tell "the truth" about any human relationship, how much more difficult it is to recall exact words, moods, and feelings lost in the past.

Today, what seems to me most valuable about *Bitter Fame* are the many quotations from letters and journals that Sylvia Plath wrote in a time that is forever "present." The poet's own writings, in other words, showed me how she was thinking at different moments while she was alive. In the archives at Smith College and Indiana, I spent many hours reading *through,* in two senses, her own descriptions of her family, her childhood, her New England society, her sexual anxieties, her ambition, her self-doubt, her jealousy, and her lifelong obsession with suicide. Then I reread her poems, giving special consideration to "Poem for a Birthday" and its ritualistic enactment of death and rebirth—the prevailing motif in her poetry and in her novel, *The Bell Jar.* Finally, after many weeks, I was able to form some idea of how those amazing *Ariel* poems had been "exacted" from her shortly before she died. I wasn't sure, of course, that my reading of Plath was "true," but it was at least plausible and sympathetic, drawn from the fulsome, sometimes painful and often contradictory evidence of her own work. If the price of being allowed to quote freely from Plath's unpublished writings was high, it was surely worth it. I can say now, too, that despite our many differences and quarrels, I am, from a distance, grateful to Olwyn Hughes for her guidance and for her generosity in handing over to me a great deal of material to which I otherwise would not have had access.

I should also make it clear that although I do not believe a perfect biography of Sylvia Plath can be written, I am not a disbeliever in the value of biography in general as a way of approaching writers and their times. Two years after *Bitter Fame* appeared, Jacqueline Rose published *The Haunting of Sylvia Plath* in which she maintained that Plath, being dead, is simply unknowable. Rose believes it is tantamount to literary sin to consider poems in a biographical context. Not a poet but a culture must be held responsible for any period's influential "texts." Sylvia Plath today, argues Rose, is no more than a ghost or fantasy of our cultural and sexual preoccupations. From this deconstructionist viewpoint (Rose also owes much to a curious mixture of feminist and Freudian theory) *Bitter Fame* is a mistake from beginning to end.

All I can say in reply is that, for me, *The Haunting of Sylvia Plath* is practically unreadable. In these deconstructionist days it is fashionable to argue that history and biography are in essence nothing but cultural inventions. I have been guilty of playing with the idea myself. Yet, to call history "fiction making" is not to say that history didn't happen or that there are no such things as facts. It is indisputable that the past has occurred. It has made our world what it is, or rather, what we know it as; we are still under an obligation to share and take care of it. If human events are always multisided and more confused than the language in which we record them, then they may be more "real" than language's necessary simplifications. In a sense it is proper to say we *invent* history. The word *invent* is derived from the Latin *invenire,* to discover. Thus we can be said to discover or uncover the past when we select from an uncountable number of happenings those few that give it order and "meaning." On the other hand, as in a scientific experiment, what we say about ourselves has in some sense to be repeatable and testable. Selection is never free, and language is not personally owned. It can be understood only socially, as a structured mode of communication. It is in this sense that the historian and biographer, by undertaking to pass on the story of "what happened," make themselves responsible for revealing—if not THE truth—at least recognizable areas of common experience. Only so many possibilities will be empirically believed; only so many stories will stand up to the test of our feelings.

Getting back to my problems with *Bitter Fame* and my reflections on biography—prompted partly by Janet Malcolm's book, partly by my own bitter experience—let me conclude by suggesting that we acknowledge quite openly that fiction making is implicit in biography making. Every biography tells a story. Neither genre is unalloyed. Much more harmful to literature are postmodernism's critical theories—inculcated in nearly every university department of English—that presuppose their own dubious axioms. Like scientists learning to accept the limitations of physical experiment, we writers must learn to work imaginatively within the limits of language. If we can't tell all the truth, we can at least tell some of it. And if none of us can be entirely right, at least we are in good company. It is as well, Janet Malcolm reminds me, to keep in mind those lovely lines from Louis MacNeice's lyric "Entirely."

If we could get the hang of it entirely
    It would take too long;
All we know is the splash of words in passing
    and falling twigs of song,
And when we try to eavesdrop on the great
    presences it is rarely
That by a stroke of luck we can appropriate
    Even a phrase entirely.

Sylvia Plath's Word Games

Everybody knows her story, and a great many readers have been excited and disturbed by her writings. How much have the dramatic details of Sylvia Plath's life contributed to the climate of awed veneration that has been generated by her poetry? What would we think of her today had she lived into her sixties, the famous author, doubtless, of eight or ten volumes of verse and a shelf of fiction?

Such questions, unanswerable as they are, come naturally to mind when we consider Sylvia Plath's published work—I mean all of it: letters, journals, prose, and poetry—from a distance of over thirty years; more years than the poet lived. Given her countless admirers and their continued interest in everything pertaining to her, it may be useful to separate out the reality of Plath's achievement from some of the hearsay that obscures it. As I see it, there are three main roots (routes) that invite exploration.

First of all, yes, we must take into consideration the circumstances of the poet's life and self-inflicted death. Although it would be simplistic to pigeonhole Plath as a "confessional" poet, there is no doubt she wrote, at least on one level, straight out of experience. She had, so her mother tells us, an extraordinary memory. She never forgot. One could say that in a Borgesian way, she was cruelly compelled to remember everything that happened to her. All her writings, therefore, teem with private images: her Winthrop childhood, Cape Cod summers, strawberry and spinach picking; movies she saw of the war; traumatic incidents, such as being admitted to a cadaver room and looking at embryos in jars of formaldehyde, together with lesser ones like observing a dead pig, watching an owl, picking a rose, sewing red material into curtains. A few ineradicable experiences—losing her father, going mad, undergoing electroconvulsive therapy, hemorrhaging when she lost her virginity, giving birth—surge again and again into her work. Unless a reader knows something of this poet's biography many of her references will be lost.

From *Poetry Review* 86, no. 4 (winter 1996).

Her private experiences, of course, would be of no importance if she had not, in poem after poem—and this is my second point—imaginatively transformed, exaggerated, and brilliantly dramatized them. Ted Hughes's interest in Christian and pre-Christian myth, augmented by her own fascinated readings of Graves, Lawrence, Jung, and Freud, profoundly affected Plath's impressionable mind. She seems really to have believed that her individual life was sacrificially in thrall to ineluctable archetypal forces. Her journal of January 3, 1959, for example, refers to the "great, stark bloody play acting itself out over and over again behind the sunny facade of our daily rituals" (*Bitter Fame,* 148). It was some such fatalistic myth, some idea of powers beyond her control that were governing her life, that, so it seems, dictated her last poems.

Once it is understood that a palingenetic scheme of death and rebirth is central to all Plath's major work, it is simple enough to identify within it a consistent system of symbols: doubles in mirrors or pools, drownings, burnings, burials, a dead ghostly father and his bees, an ever-present, bitterly resented mother, nullifying statues, shape-changing witches, and puppet master of them all, the ambiguous figure of the moon—the bald nurse cum disquieting muse of her private mythology. Many of these recurring signatures are linked, moreover, to colors, such as red (life), white (deathly stasis), black (annihilation), green (spring, but also poison), and so forth. Those who are fascinated by the myth will find in Judith Kroll's *Chapters in a Mythology* (1976) a reliable guide to its iconography. Kroll stresses, too, the poet's immense debt to the visual arts. One way to teach Plath's poems would be to ask students to make paintings of them.

Finally, though, we must acknowledge that Sylvia Plath, from her earliest years, put her writing on a par with her life, and when we turn to that writing, one of the first things we notice is how much this self-making maker of myths was indebted to other writers with whom she put herself to school. All her life she was a deeply serious, fanatically obsessed student. Sometimes consciously, sometimes unconsciously, she "hooked" images and ideas from books she intimately knew (many of them children's books) or from literature she had scrupulously studied, underlined, and memorized. How deeply she was indebted to T. S. Eliot I hope partially to demonstrate today. But she was equally indebted to the work of D. H. Lawrence, Dylan Thomas, Yeats, Auden, and Theodore Roethke, while technically she imitated James Joyce, whose tricks with words she could perform as well as he could.

Perhaps it is a measure of Plath's originality that the loot she indefatigably appropriated from her literary forebears has never been much noticed. One of her objects, I'm pretty sure, was to contain or reformulate the classics of the past in a bid, like Eliot's, to refresh and remold the tradition. Nothing if not a modernist, Sylvia Plath, in my view, deserves fame for her literary skill, for technical cleverness, musicality, economy of diction, and a keen wit—achievements that would eventually have made her name as a mature writer had not psychological illness and a too personally interpreted myth driven her to kill herself. Rather than concentrate further on the personal tragedy of this remarkable poet, I hope scholars will find time in the future to study her language and the way in which her writings tie into and reinforce major themes in *her* work and *our* time. For there is no denying that twentieth-century high culture, which began so hopefully in an era of innovative triumph, now seems itself on the point of committing suicide out of what looks like pique, or an attack of fin de siècle exhaustion.

I was first alerted to the amount of T. S. Eliot that Plath incorporated into her writing by a not-very-complimentary review. *Bitter Fame,* wrote the reviewer, culpably failed to connect an abandoned title for Plath's first book of poems with Eliot's "Ash Wednesday." True enough, "The Devil of the Stairs" comes from part 3 of Eliot's poem: "At the first turning of the second stair / I turned and saw below / The same shape twisted on the banister / Under the vapour in the fetid air / Struggling with the devil of the stairs."

At around the same time (1958–59) Plath also considered borrowing a phrase from Eliot's *Four Quartets* and using it as the title of a short story. The story was finally called "The Daughters of Blossom Street." "The Earth Our Hospital," however, initially struck the author as appropriate—taken from Eliot's lyric for Good Friday ("East Coker," part 4): "The whole earth is our hospital / Endowed by the ruined millionaire." Since *millionaire* crops up in "Stopped Dead" as well as (rather exaggeratedly) in a good many of Plath's letters and journals, it is possible that Eliot helped to furnish her mind with the word—along with other Plathic familiars: the surgeon, the nurse, Adam, mental wires (nerves), fever, roses, flames, and the eucharistic blood and flesh of Eliot's hymn. Very likely Sylvia Plath knew part 4 of "East Coker" by heart.

In it, Eliot's "wounded surgeon," a figure of Christ, operates on the body of Christianity lying "distempered" under his "bleeding hands." The second stanza introduces "a dying nurse" whose care it is to keep Christianity's disease instrumental to its health, reminding us of "Adam's curse" and insisting that "to be restored, our sickness must grow worse." It is at this point that the famous lines about "the earth our hospital" occur, "endowed by the ruined millionaire"—that is, by a God bankrupt in the world he created, who ordains that "if we do well" we will die (and thus be saved) of the "absolute paternal care" that has given us life. Finally, two paradoxical stanzas reassert the palingenetic myth at the heart of the Christian mystery. It is striking how Plath-like Eliot's succession of images are.

> The chill ascends from feet to knees,
> The *fever* sings in *mental wires.*
> If to be warmed, then I must freeze
> And quake in frigid purgatorial *fires*
> Of which the *flame is roses,* and the *smoke is briars.*

Plathian words are italicized. For Plath's burning roses, see also George Macdonald's children's tale *The Princess and the Goblin;* for briars, read hooks. Eliot continues

> The *dripping blood* our only drink,
> The *bloody flesh* our only *food* . . .

Of course we can't single out Eliot's hymn, in its unmistakable Christian context, as the only source of Plath's imagery. Roses and—or as—flames, usually with sexual implications, run all through the Western poetic tradition, as Plath well knew. Yet, though not specifically Christian, the terms of Plath's death-and-resurrection myth hardly eschewed Christian iconography. Remember how often she had recourse to the "Communion tablet"—even while rejecting it. If you trace the Communion wafer through her work, you soon see that it stands for a whole class of words having to do with eating (accepting) as likewise and significantly for its opposite, revulsion (rejecting). In "Medusa," for example:

> Who do you think you are?
> A Communion wafer? Blubbery Mary?

Later, she cried out in "Totem," "Let us eat it like Plato's afterbirth, / Let us eat it like Christ" (Christ, here, must be Plato's afterbirth); and in "Mystic" "What is the remedy? / "The pill of the Communion tablet . . . ?"

"Adam's curse" would have been familiar to Plath from Yeats as well as Eliot—as in "Side of green Adam" in "Purdah." See also "mud . . . / Thick, red and slipping. It is Adam's side" in "Getting There." Ted Hughes says Plath knew that the name Adam means "red earth," so it's pretty certain she consciously made a connection between the biblical reference and the blood-colored Devon soil from which Eve/Plath in "Getting There" is being (re)born. Indeed, there was no reason why this poet should not make use of every bit of mythopoetical language she could lay her hands on. Eliot believed that to bring other poets back to life was one of the perennial tasks of modern poetry. Even a comparatively early poem such as "The Stones" can be considered, in one of its aspects, as a comment on and criticism of Eliot that brings a she-Christ back to life in a questioning, perhaps even skeptical, frame of reference.

> Love is the uniform of my *bald nurse,* [skull of the risen god/goddess]
> Love is the bone and sinew of my *curse.* [Adam's/Eve's fall]
> The vase, reconstructed, houses
> The *elusive rose.* [redemption through love]
>
> (My italics)

Plath, of course, was recounting her own emergence from spiritual death and purgatorial suffering. It would have been natural for her to feminize and adapt the older poet's rituals for the ceremony of her rebirth. In her last poem, "Edge," the rose recurs, together with the bald nurse-moon, but here the flower is killed by the skull-like moon's crackling blacks (its eye-and-mouth sockets) that, despite poetry and its healing "blood jet," are dragging the poet for ever out of the rose garden.

> She has folded
>
> Them [her children] back into her body as petals
> Of a rose close when the garden
>
> Stiffens and odors bleed
> From the sweet, deep throats of the night flower.
>
> The moon has nothing to be sad about,
> Staring from her hood of bone.
>
> She is used to this sort of thing.
> Her blacks crackle and drag.

"The Bee Meeting," too, makes undercover reference to Eliot. Here is the "sacred grove" transformed into a garden rank with hawthorn that "etherizes" its children (as in that famous line from "Prufrock") followed by a passage describing ordinary neighbors and beekeepers as ritually attired priests or celebrants. Simultaneously, they are robed patients gathered in expectation of a surgeon who will perform a vital, yet almost certainly fatal, operation.

> They are leading me to the shorn grove, the circle of hives
> Is it the hawthorn that smells so sick?
> The barren body of hawthorn, etherizing its children.
>
> Is it some operation that is taking place?
> It is the surgeon my neighbors are waiting for.
> This apparition in a green helmet,
> Shining gloves and white suit.

Ted Hughes testifies that Plath everywhere combined Eliot's sacrificial myths with those of D. H. Lawrence, whose fable "The Man Who Died" had made a powerful impression upon her when she was at Cambridge. "I was the woman who died," she wrote in August 1953, referring to Lawrence's resurrected, sexual Christ cum Osiris, "and I came in touch through Sassoon [a former lover] with that flaming of life, that resolute fury of existence."

In the pre-Ariel poems, Eliot's rhythm and diction tended to overlay Lawrence's thematic matter. (Though it could be argued, too, that Plath's more plaintive Ariel voice to some extent echoes Lawrence's in his last poems.) Not only did Plath in "The Bee Meeting" snip bits from Eliot's vocabulary; she adopted, in the interrogative mood, the very syntax and sounds of "Prufrock," mixing it with echoes from the vegetation ceremony in "East Coker." Listen to the short "i" combined with "s" and "t" that spikes the rhetorical questions in "The Bee Meeting": *is it, is it?* straight out of "Prufrock": "Oh, do not ask, 'what is it?' / Let us go and make our visit." Further examples of hissing noises are rife in Plath's mockery (perhaps) of Eliot's portentousness in her poem "A Birthday Present."

> What *is this,* behind this veil, *is it* ugly, is it beautiful?
> *It is* shimmering, *has it* breasts, *has it* edges?
>
> . . . "*Is this* the one I am to appear for,
> *Is this* the elect one, the one with black eye-pits and a scar?"
>
> (My italics)

"A Birthday Present," indeed, seems an absolute present to the feminists among us, who will correctly read it as an attack on the entire patriarchal tradition. Lies, lies, lies, the poem cries, like the rest of history. How cleverly, though, Plath plays with her pastiche of Eliot's tone. I take "it" in this poem to stand for some terrible sacrificial truth hidden in the veils of social orthodoxy (present giving). The conclusion recasts Eliot's Christian myth in Plath's characteristically iconoclastic mold. Veils and shroudings are among her recurrent images, habitual distress signals belonging to the Plathian code.

> Only let down the veil, the veil, the veil.
> If it were death
> I would admire the deep gravity of it, its timeless eyes.
> I would know you were serious.

The way in which Plath used signs and sounds to suggest connections she liked to make with literary tradition—even when she attacked it—was brought to my attention by an English scholar, C. G. Richmond. To be fair, she, not I, should be presenting a paper on Sylvia Plath's word games, for Connie Richmond—who first studied Plath as a mature student about twenty years ago—believes that all Plath's poems were constructed according to a system encoded in their texts, a cryptic game based on Roget's *Thesaurus* that, given persistence and a gift for detection, can be discovered by any devotee patient enough to follow a trail of deliberately laid clues. I'm not sure I go along with all Richmond's ideas, but they are certainly interesting. She suggests, for instance, that Plath often used sounds to suggest names for fictional characters. Disguises for Eliot would include "Elly Higgenbottom" and "Elaine" in *The Bell Jar,* "Ella Mason and her Eleven Cats," "Ellen" in "The Baby Sitters," "Ellen" in the short story "Day of Success" and "Nellie Meehan" in the story "All the Dead Dears." Recurrent in Plath's writing are sounds such as *el, eli, li, lee;* that is, em*bell*ish, bell, smell, *del*icate, sleep—all cryptograms for Eliot.

Well, perhaps. Plath did admire James Joyce, and many of her early poems are indeed cleverly executed Joycean exercises. Later poems, however, give evidence that her borrowings were more straightforward. The opening of "Poem for a Birthday," written at Yaddo in 1959, echoes, for example, one of Eliot's "Choruses from *The Rock.*" Here is Plath's "Who?":

> The month of flowering's finished. The fruit's in,
> Eaten or rotten. I am all mouth.
> October's the month for storage.

And here is Eliot's second "Chorus":

> Of all that was done in the past, you eat the fruit, either rotten
> or ripe.
> And the Church must be forever building, and always decaying,
> and always being restored.

It's hard not to conclude that Plath has taken Eliot's Christian symbol literally and used "fruit" as a building block in her own mythology. "All mouth" in the same sequence we know was borrowed from Jung, while the structural "feel" of the poem shadows Theodore Roethke's "The Lost Son," which Plath read seemingly for the first time at Yaddo that autumn.

Whatever her debt to Eliot and Roethke, "Poem for a Birthday" surely represents Plath's first serious attempt to transmute her experience of madness and the "death" and "rebirth" that followed her 1953 suicide attempt into art. And clearly, as a work of art, the seven-part sequence exemplifies the modernist practice of piecing together a text out of copious borrowings from the culture's word-hoard. Plath also, of course, added to the mix some goodly chunks of her own. Defoe's dragonlike, disease-carrying monsters of infected breath from *A Journal of the Plague Year* become inhabitants of the vast lake of dreams Plath invokes in "Johnny Panic and the Bible of Dreams"—and that dream lake, as Ted Hughes confirms, was an actual nightmare Plath experienced in terrifying detail.

Sometimes Sylvia Plath's almost perfect memory got in her way. In her journal of 1959, for example, she complained of remembering too much. "Lines occur to me and stop dead; 'The tiger lily's spotted throat.' And then it is an echo of Eliot's 'The tiger in the tiger pit' to the syllable and the consonance." True enough, Eliot's "Lines for an Old Man" begins "The tiger in the tiger pit / Is not more irritable than I, / The whipping tail is not more still, / Than when I smell the enemy / Writhing in the essential blood / or dangling from the friendly tree." Light verse? Nevertheless, Eliot's black joke puts in a prior claim, not only for Plath's tiger, but for the gigantic class of words she associated with blood; as also for her (partly) Tarot-inspired hanging man, and her madness. Like all modern poets, she confronted the aggravating, sometimes insuperable problem of writing in a tradition in which almost every word is a hand-me-down.

The tiger has a long history in literature. Lewis Carroll's tiger lily in *Through the Looking Glass* would seem to be one source; but there was Blake's "Tyger," too, not to mention Shakespeare's Henry V advising his soldiers to imitate the tiger at Agincourt. Plath, like Eliot before her, would have been familiar with Kipling's fables and verses. Yet, despite many precedents, Plath did not hesitate to work the tiger lily, at least, into that unforgettable and very beautiful poem to her baby son, "The Night Dances."

Paying close attention to Plath's literary sources and verbal facility directs attention away from her personal drama and focuses it on her very considerable wit. A vein of wit runs through all her work, though in the *Ariel* poems (note that her title again relates to a group of Eliot's poems) it tends to convert to cynicism, or sometimes, as in "Medusa," to cruel, raucous attack. When she first read "Daddy" and "Lady Lazarus" to A. Alvarez she described them—to his amazement—as "light verse." Much of her early work—poems she wrote while she was at Cambridge, for instance—can be understood as tough-worded humor. Look, for example, at "Natural History"—number 56 in the *Collected Poems*.

That lofty monarch, Monarch Mind,
Blue-blooded in coarse country reigned;
Though he bedded in ermine, gorged on roast,
Pure Philosophy his love engrossed:
While subjects hungered, empty-pursed,
With stars, with angels, he conversed

Till, sick of their ruler's godling airs,
In one body those earthborn commoners
Rose up and put royal nerves to the rack:
King Egg-Head saw his domain crack,
His crown usurped by the low brow
Of the base, barbarous Prince Ow.

The whole poem is a joke based on the old saw about the philosopher who couldn't reason away his toothache. Its anti–intellectualism is perhaps a trifle crude, owing something, maybe, to Yeats, something to the Elizabethans she was studying at Cambridge at the time, a good deal, perhaps, to Ted Hughes and Lucas Myers, with whom she regularly exchanged poems.

C. G. Richmond believes that Plath's texts all hide a "serious discussion of something else" that ought to be looked for when they seem superficially obscure. Puns and portmanteau words, she thinks, conceal references to what is often called "something else" outright: "Hard gods were there, nothing else. / Still he thumbed out *something else*" ("The Hermit at Outermost House"); "*Something else* / Hauls me through air . . . / Dead hands, dead stringencies ("Ariel"); "All day, gluing my church of burnt matchsticks, / I dream of *someone else* entirely" ("The Jailor"); "This is not death, it is *something safer*" ("Flute Notes from a Reedy Pond").

Now, it may be, as Richmond suggests, that this "something else" is nothing less than the entire body (or canon) of Western literature to which Plath knew her work would some day belong. On the other hand, a more likely source of this reiterated "something else" was Plath's continual complaint in her journals of dissatisfaction with what she was writing. "These poems do not live: it's a sad diagnosis," she wrote in the poem "Stillborn." Ted Hughes is right, I think, when he suggests that before she secured in "Elm" the Ariel voice that began to emerge in "Poem for a Birthday" she was infuriatingly gnawed by a feeling that she ought to be writing about *something else.*

So without entirely agreeing with Richmond, we can be grateful for her close readings, particularly of early poems, that show us how important "something else" always was to Sylvia Plath. When she was in college she could well have associated "something else" with poetry she judged to be more successful than her own. We know she carried the poems of Dylan Thomas around with her "like sacred talismans." And here again, the relationship between Plath's often contorted syntax and that of Dylan Thomas—an even more potent influence on her early work than Eliot—could do with some careful looking into. Equally, when we read in Plath "I Am Vertical / But I would rather be horizontal," it's as well to remember how familiar she was with the poems of W. H. Auden, who dedicated his *Poems, 1927–1931* to Christopher Isherwood with this wry quatrain.

> Let us honour if we can
> The vertical man.
> Though we value none
> But the horizontal one.

I am suggesting, in other words, that Plath took her ideas of what poetry should be from the influential modernists she admired: Joyce, on whom she would have written her college thesis had she not broken down in 1953, as well as T. S. Eliot, D. H. Lawrence, Dylan Thomas, W. H. Auden, and even Ezra Pound—whose "Ballad of the Goodly *Fere,*" meaning mate or brother in middle English, just may have induced her to play with its phonic twin, *fear,* in the chorus of "Johnny Panic."

The only thing to love is Fear itself.
Love of Fear is the beginning of wisdom.
The only thing to love is Fear itself
May Fear and Fear and Fear be everywhere.

Love of "fear" would then, subliminally, imply brotherly love, and if so, the rhyming chant might appear to be more palatable than we had supposed. I myself believe such a reading to be well wide of the mark. Fear, the "panic bird" of the stories and poems that preceded the bold confrontations of *Ariel,* was too much this poet's presiding genius to admit of much wordplay. But Richmond's approach should not be ignored, either. She shows us again and again how for Plath language was a relished source of enjoyment as well as a means of charting the tragedy of an attempted salvation.

In these late days of the century, our ideas of what Plath intended to do in poetry have in many instances been distorted by postmodernist language-theory and political emotion. A general desire to establish an independent women's tradition, for example, has persuaded some women critics to make pronouncements about Plath's psyche, personal habits, and sexual orientation on wholly imaginary evidence. If Sylvia Plath was a major poet, she was not just a major woman poet, nor would she have wanted, I believe, to be enthroned in a women's ghetto.

True, in her last year she indeed turned the cannon of her scholarship and prosodic skill against the "male tradition" she had up until then energetically emulated. To do this, she made use of every bit of traditional lore she could lay hands on, visibly rejoicing in wordplay and sly literary references. What any and every aspiring woman poet ought to learn from Sylvia Plath, it seems to me, is how to overhear, imitate, play variations on, and eventually transmute the English tradition in a wholly original and affective way. Sylvia Plath wasn't *democratic* about her feminism any more than Emily Dickinson or Elizabeth Bishop—or even Marianne Moore, who went out of her way, at one time, to slap down the ambitious young Plath. I should like to suggest that closely studying Plath's language, vocabulary, and literary borrowings, as Richmond has, unnoticed and unacknowledged over the years, is a rewarding and enriching approach to her work. In a recorded interview at Yale (April 18, 1958) Sylvia Plath described the way she herself set about writing poetry.

Technically I like to be extremely musical and lyrical, with a singing sound. I don't like poetry that just throws itself away in prose. I think there should be a kind of constriction and a kind of music, too. And again, I like the idea of managing to get wit in with the idea of seriousness, and contrasts, ironies, and I like visual images, and I like just good mouthfuls of sound which have meaning. . . . I lean very strongly toward forms that are, I suppose, quite rigid in comparison certainly to free verse. I'm much happier when I know that all my sounds are echoing in different ways throughout the poem.

Well, there you have it. Together with her literary inheritance those "good mouthfuls of sound," that wit with seriousness, and the musical constrictions and forms of Plath's poetry will take us all, I believe, a long way along the road to understanding—and enjoying it.

The Iceberg and the Ship

On Elizabeth Bishop

Elizabeth Bishop's poetry is an acquired taste, but one that easily turns other poets into addicts. John Ashbery said of her once that she was a "writer's writer's writer"—a description that hardly explains the breadth of her appeal. In the early 1960s, when I first discovered "The Fish" in a college anthology, she was chiefly praised for the finely observed details she "painted" into her poems. Who else would liken a hooked fish to ancient rose-patterned wallpaper, or imagine its flesh "packed in like feathers" and its swim-bladder "like a big peony"?

No wonder that in England, during the 1970s, the so-called Martian poets hailed Elizabeth Bishop as a predecessor. If Bishop herself acknowledged a predecessor, it was Marianne Moore and her delightful homespun fables full of moral animals and eccentric admonitions. As is well known, Moore personally encouraged the young Bishop and helped her to publish. Today, Bishop's reputation stands higher than Moore's—though both were lauded by that most discerning critic of the midcentury, Randall Jarrell. Jarrell's assessment of Bishop still seems just, although he could not have foreseen at the time the autobiographical turn Bishop's later work would take. In 1963, Jarrell wrote:

> Her poems are quiet, truthful, sad, funny, most marvelously individual poems; they have a sound, a feel, a whole moral and physical atmosphere, different from anything else I know. They are honest, modest, minutely observant, masterly. . . . Her best poems . . . remind one of Vuillard or even, sometimes, of Vermeer.[1]

But Jarrell went on to qualify this out-and-out praise in a way, I suspect, few critics would today. He did not, for instance, claim for Elizabeth Bishop the distinction of greatness.

This chapter originated as the Kathleen Banks Lecture 1995, on the writings of Elizabeth Bishop, given at the University of Loughborough, England, November 28, 1995. Reprinted from *Michigan Quarterly Review* 35, no. 4 (fall 1996).

Of late, Elizabeth Bishop has become something of a cult figure among the literati of America and England. She has been taken up, worshiped, almost deified, not only because her exquisite poetry and prose make for immensely pleasurable reading—who can resist that tone of "large, grave tenderness and sorrowing amusement" that Robert Lowell characterized so accurately—but because the private circumstances of her restless, often unhappy life have been made available for inspection through the publication of two biographies and a profusion of letters. A poet can suffer no worse fate than being celebrated for the wrong reasons. How much better if her loving editors and critics, to borrow one of Bishop's own phrases, had kept some things to themselves. This essay will eschew, therefore, all redundant considerations of Elizabeth Bishop's sexual orientation and her by now overpublicized addiction to alcohol. Unhappy events in her life did affect her poetry, but chiefly as she met and overcame them through her art.

"The art of losing isn't hard to master," she wrote in her late and only villanelle, "though it may look like (*Write* it!) like disaster." The personal losses written *of* in "One Art" are simultaneously, almost cheerily, written *off*. The poet earns sympathy by diverting attention away from morbid particulars and catching it instead in a generalized, witty reflection on the human condition. We all lose everything, eventually, but if we can *write* it, the loss (even of our lives, presumably) isn't a disaster. *Ars longa, vita brevis*—but how amusingly put!

Generalizing or gaily philosophizing in this way was far from Elizabeth Bishop's usual practice; she mostly built up her poems detail by detail until they collected themselves into an affirmative revelation. "The Fish" ends in a victory just as meaningful as "One Art," though it is brought about differently by an accumulation of wonderfully observed minutia.

> I stared and stared
> and victory filled up
> the little rented boat,
> from the pool of bilge . . .
> to the bailer rusted orange,
> the sun-cracked thwarts,
> the oarlocks on their strings,

the gunnels—until everything
was rainbow, rainbow, rainbow!
And I let the fish go.

It is to such revelations, to such—can I say epiphanic show-
ings forth?—as they occur time and again in Elizabeth Bishop's
poetry that her most sensitive readers will probably respond.
Before looking at her poems, though, let me risk advancing
some ideas that may help us to approach Bishop with enriched
understanding. As David Kalstone observed as long ago as 1977,
Elizabeth Bishop is hard to "place." In any overview of modern
American poetry, she seems never exactly to fit the available
pigeonholes. When, in 1962, Twayne publishers signed me up to
write a study of her work, "placing her" presented a difficulty. (I
hadn't then realized that one needn't always place poets; and
such a thing as a women's tradition never then occurred to me.)
I think now, however, that she can be placed well enough; her
work surely locates itself in the mainstream of American letters.
Late in 1963, Bishop herself helped me with a remark casually
thrown off in a letter:

> it is odd how often I feel myself to be a late-late Post World War
> I generation member, rather than a member of the Post World
> War II generation. . . . But I also feel that [Robert Lowell] and I
> in our very different ways are both descendants from the Tran-
> scendentalists.[2]

Part of this passage made good sense. Bishop had gone to
Europe in 1935, earlier than most of her contemporaries, and
then (or maybe before then) she had come under the spell of
the surrealists. At Vassar College, her literary heroes (apart from
George Herbert and Father Hopkins) were American poets of
an older generation: Frost, Cummings, Eliot, Hart Crane, Wil-
liam Carlos Williams, Wallace Stevens, and especially Marianne
Moore. It seemed natural to me—and Bishop certainly ap-
proved at the time—to write of her as a late, sophisticated mod-
ernist. In another letter she readily admitted to being a snob. At
Vassar she had been caricatured in the college magazine as one
of "The Higher Type." She seemed to be rather proud of this.
Yet she said, too, that she had always wanted to write popular
songs. "Songs for a Colored Singer," in her first book, were

written with Billie Holiday in mind; later her ballad "The Burglar of Babylon" was genuinely popular in Brazil.

Well, it came as no surprise that an avant-garde modernist should be enthralled with folk music. What did surprise me in the 1960s was that casually dropped remark about being descended from the Transcendentalists. I couldn't at the time see that Bishop's writings had anything in common with Emerson or Thoreau—except a profound feeling for nature. Any notion of an Oversoul, though, or of a Wordsworthian Divine Presence in nature seemed alien to the poet's scintillating sophistication. Transcendence, I thought, meant a *higher* state of being, a reality more elevated than our mortal condition. It wasn't until much later, after *Geography III* appeared in 1976, that it occurred to me that a good enough poet, a poet who had inherited Hopkins's eye and Herbert's instinct to praise whatever in life was "new, tender, quick," might well look for transcendence (or its equivalent) *in,* or *under,* the natural appearances of the world—and find it there, too.

Once a reader has been alerted to the otherness, to the mysterious animation that warms the brilliant surface of almost all Bishop's writing, the mixture in her first two books of dreamlike surrealism with exact geographical description doesn't seem so odd. The poet herself, in a famous letter, spoke frankly of the pleasure she took in living and doing things in the "real" world, while being aware, always, of its inherent, even more "real" yet impenetrable mystery.[3]

"Yes," she wrote, "I agree with you. There is no 'split' [between consciousness and unconsciousness]. Dreams, works of art (some), glimpses of the always-more-successful surrealism of everyday life, unexpected moments of empathy (is it?), catch a peripheral vision of whatever it is one can never really see full-face, but that seems enormously important." As an overall summation of what we may call Elizabeth Bishop's *quest;* as a plain statement of the "importance" she was looking for when she set off on her travels, exterior and interior, those few sentences are as revealing as any we have.

Nevertheless, while alerting ourself to the energies and revelations latent in all Bishop's writing, it does seem possible to detect a "split," in a sense other than psychological, between the poems of her first two books, written before 1952, when, after years of dislocation, she settled in Brazil, and those written once she was established there—and later.

Typical of her early work is "The Imaginary Iceberg," which does indeed treat of a "split" between a visionary iceberg—call it a dream of natural perfection, or an idea of perfected design, artless art—and a ship full of presumably flawed sailors/artists who, says the poet, would give their eyes and even their lives to "own" the iceberg. Contemplating the dichotomy, the poet (at least in 1934) appeared to take the side of the iceberg. "We'd rather have the iceberg than the ship, / although it meant the end of travel." This rather astounding statement occurs twice in the first stanza.

The poet then goes on to suggest that the iceberg "pastures" on its snows the way (possibly) a work of art feeds on the imagination of the artist. Promising its watchers an almost mathematical spectacle of unified truth and beauty, such an "imaginary" self-created object signifies, it seems to me, not exactly the imagination but something that embodies the *independent nature of the imagined.* Indivisible, dazzling, existing only for itself, the iceberg's ahuman otherness is set up as something "we'd" rather "own" than our admittedly safer "ship of fools"—or perhaps, as Isaiah Berlin has it, our "bent timber of humanity." The iceberg behooves our souls because it is self-made and pure, godlike, incorruptible, not of human making. I can't see how to read this poem in any light other than Transcendentalist. It seems to me openly aspiring and dualistic, for all its updated surrealistic trappings.

Compare "The Imaginary Iceberg" with Bishop's poems of the 1950s and early 1960s in *Questions of Travel,* and we immediately notice a shift of emphasis. Bishop published a number of controlled, delicately moralized descriptions like "The Fish" and "At the Fishhouses" in her two first collections, while an acute empathy with social anomie had given her "Cootchie" and "Faustina," too. But she had mixed such poems of wise "sorrowing amusement" (and not a little anger, viz. "Roosters") with surrealist offerings such as "The Man Moth," "The Monument," and the philosophically entertaining "Gentleman of Shalott." Her early books look, in retrospect, like a showcase of everything she technically could perform.

The first section of her third book, in contrast, consists of eleven plainer poems set in Brazil—one of which, "Arrival in Santos"—she appropriately borrowed from *A Cold Spring*. All of these either describe Brazil as a place traveled to and awesomely observed, or they evoke native Brazilians who (not excepting her armadillo) have been "colonialized" and exploited but who nevertheless embodied for her the value and, really, the sacredness of life. The poet has steered off, in other words, away from the iceberg, into warmer, sadder waters in company with the poorest of the sailors aboard the human ship. The third section of *Questions of Travel*, called "Elsewhere," returns in the same spirit to Nova Scotia and to scenes from the poet's childhood. Between these two main sections, Bishop artfully placed the finest poem (possibly) she ever wrote, which happens to have been written in prose. "In the Village" tells, with almost no fictional distortion, the story of her widowed mother's emotional breakdown and permanent departure for a mental hospital in Dartmouth, Nova Scotia—an event that happened in the summer of 1916. Elizabeth Bishop at the time was five years old.

Everyone who is interested in Elizabeth Bishop will know "In the Village," now a classic, which first came out in the *New Yorker* in December 1953. Among many critics who have studied it, Victoria Harrison has given us a particularly helpful account of its origins in an unpublished fragment Bishop wrote shortly after leaving Vassar in 1934.[4] For our purposes, we need note only the simplicity and power of the story itself—which indeed is, as Bishop herself said, nearly all true. "In the Village" is set within brackets, as it were, of two contrasting sounds: the mother's demented scream, which still, perhaps, stains those pure blue skies of Nova Scotia, and the beautiful "clang!" of Nate's (the blacksmith's) hammer as he shapes a horseshoe in the nearby forge. From the beginning we realize that to her apprehensive child, this disturbed mother—who has come home and gone away, and then come back and then again disappeared, and now is back once more—represents nothing but uncertainty, chaos, and finally a shame the child acutely feels, picking it up from her aunts and grandmother without knowing what it is. The blacksmith, on the other hand, embodies the rooted order and beauty of a "home" (for Great Village and all it represents is "home" in the story) that the mother—who is perceived only negatively—has been unable to provide.

"In the Village" must be understood as the pivotal *fact* of Elizabeth Bishop's lifework. It forms a bridge, that is, between her work and her life that was not accessible to her earlier—for all her early poems' fascination and charm. For in this one short real-life story, the psychic wound, the shadowy pain that one senses so often under or between Bishop's lines, is made explicit. At the same time, in the same story, it is overcome. As the child's world is shattered by the mother's scream, it is simultaneously healed by the "clang" of the blacksmith's hammer. "Oh beautiful sound strike again."

Nate, the blacksmith, like Bishop herself, is, of course, a *maker;* but even more than this, the story casts him as a magician, a green knight whose role is to conjure up the "good" powers of nature that, in Bishop's *work* at least, always succeed in vanquishing the "bad" ones, such as those called forth by the scream. The story, with Nate as its hearth-god, ends in triumph, even as it leaves us with the certain knowledge that the child has lost her mother forever. The Transcendentalist, nearly Wordsworthian, tones of the last page seem to me quite unmistakable, although so much childlike, exact village detail has paved the way to it that a reader scarcely remarks the charged invocation of the conclusion.

> Now there is no scream. Once there was one and it settled slowly down to earth one hot summer afternoon; or did it float up, into that dark, too dark, blue sky? But surely it has gone away, forever. It sounds like a bell buoy out at sea. It is the elements speaking: earth, air, fire, water. All those other things—clothes, crumbling postcards, broken china; things damaged and lost, sickened or destroyed; even the frail almost-lost scream—are they too frail for us to hear their voices long, too mortal?
>
> Nate!
> Oh, beautiful sound, strike again!

This ending, unrestrainedly romantic as it is, creates an effect that seems a whole century away from the wry approval the poet later accorded to the mastery of the art of losing.

In the late 1950s, Bishop's friend Robert Lowell astounded his fellow poets by renouncing the rhetorical style of his early quasi-metaphysical verse, and instead turning inward to address his own troubles. Inevitably, in the course of psychoanalysis and self-questioning, he discovered his true subject in the annals of his family. Bishop must have felt encouraged to look in the same direction. For there, in her own family history, her "true subject" assuredly lay. "In the Village" is an almost exact account of Gertrude Bulmer Bishop's mental breakdown and the enduring effect it had on her extra sensitive five-year-old daughter. In writing this story, I believe, Bishop crossed a sort of Rubicon. She began to allow herself to remember the childhood trauma that probably made her (or helped to make her) what she was. At the same time, she began to see how her memories—all clear as a moving picture to her—could be recast as art.

Looking, then, once again at the poems, important differences between early and later Bishop begin to emerge. Compare, for instance, her two sestinas: "A Miracle for Breakfast," written in New York in the 1930s, at the time of the Great Depression, and the poem simply called "Sestina," published in 1965. It is possible to pick out, in the first sestina, the social material of soup lines and unemployment that Bishop says inspired the poem. Yet "A Miracle for Breakfast" can hardly be called a "political poem" as we speak of "politicized" literature today. It is far too abstract; too mysterious, too bouncy. Reading it, one hardly feels pity for the recipients of the crumbs and drops of coffee on offer; for doesn't the poem tell us that these are the makings of a miracle?

I have always read "A Miracle for Breakfast" as a secular enactment of the Eucharist and at the same time as the lightest possible sermon on the gift of imagination. If you *look* hard enough at the free crumb life gives you, your imagination may turn it into a beautiful villa out of which floats the smell of hot coffee. A baroque plaster balcony made of bird droppings may run along the front; you can see it all "with one eye close to the crumb." This is the sort of miracle the English poet and latterday Romantic Peter Redgrove would recognize right away as a daily occurrence. The crumb becomes an entire, imaginary world—something like the iceberg, but more human, more like the bread of life. If "We'd rather have the iceberg than the ship" suggests that we'd rather have imagination's coldest dream (as embodied in art?) than the flawed vessel of our daily existence, then "A Miracle for Breakfast" puts bread and coffee in the iceberg's place. And although this sestina's final tercet ends on a downbeat, with the vision fading and "the miracle working on the wrong balcony," at least we know the miracle is happening *somewhere.* Earthly transformations, to the eye of imagination, can occur, if not always where and when we want them.

Moving even closer to the dailiness of reality, "Sestina"— untitled because the poet found it impossible to stamp so painful a recollection with a name?—altogether refuses to indulge the imagination at the expense of what happened. Sestinas are usually technical exhibition pieces; "Look what I can do!" they say, showing off. But one sees right away that this one is different: sober, stoic, painful, pretty obviously drawn from the poet's memory, however carefully she has avoided the trap of a first-person singular pronoun.

Helen Vendler, in a famous essay,[5] alerted us to the innocuous effect of all the line endings save one: tears. House, grandmother, child, stove, almanac are all homely words; what could be safer? But tears manipulate the poem. Though there are miracles on offer here, too, they are not marvelous enough to dry up the tears. The almanac has foretold them, the grandmother drinks them. When the moons fall down from the almanac into the flowerbed in the child's picture, they are transformed into tears. The Little Marvel Stove (notice the double entendre) should be able to cheer up the grandmother, but it can't because it's crying hot tears itself. In the end, as in "Some Dreams They Forgot" and "Songs for a Colored Singer," the tears are planted like seeds. These are the seeds that fate, in the guise of the almanac, will bring to fruition in the future, as the homeless child draws yet "another inscrutable house."

This later sestina, held so close to the poet's chest that it yields its miracles only tear by tear, as it were, disappointed me when I first encountered it. It was part of the manuscript of *Questions of Travel* that Elizabeth Bishop had her agent send me in the summer of 1963. At the time, I made little of it. It seemed lacking in energy and invention. Its homely pathos I thought gratuitous, even sentimental. It struck me as less attractive, less wise, and much less fun than "A Miracle for Breakfast," and I judged it to be an experiment in a flat, low-key style that I wasn't sure worked. Today, I believe it to be one of Bishop's best, most subtle achievements—which shows how long it takes, sometimes, for a fine poem to reach even its most sympathetic readers.

In speaking of a "split" between Bishop's early and later poems, and of another between a symbolic iceberg and a symbolic ship in her work—the iceberg representing those rare, most precious glimpses of something numinous she can never see full face, and the ship, a life-saving ordinariness, usually domestic—I am suggesting no more than an approach. Please don't carry away some dualistic formula. Nothing is ever formulistic in Elizabeth Bishop's writing; that's one of its strengths. Any polarities we find only bind her work together; her division splits only to come together in a new perspective.

In a curious early poem derived from George Herbert's "Love Unknown" (with something of Baudelaire in it, too) Bishop pictures herself "dead, and meditating" upon a grave or bed. After a time, her "cold heart" is divided by a "slight young weed" that pushes through it. The weed grows and splits the heart, from which gushes a flood of water. Two rivers separate and cascade over her ribs into the earth, almost sweeping away the weed, which scatters a few drops of water on the face of the sleeper (corpse). Her eyes then perceive that each drop—like the breadcrumb in "A Miracle for Breakfast"—contains an illuminated scene, and that the stream itself is made of images: "As if a river should carry all / the scenes that it had once reflected / shut in its waters, and not floating / on momentary surfaces." In the end, the speaker asks the weed, "What are you doing there?" The weed lifts its dripping head and answers, "I grow . . . but to divide your heart again."

This imaginary weed that splits the poet's dead heart can be seen to play a fanciful variation on the theme of the imaginary iceberg. The dead, self-sufficient heart is forever doomed to be split—and relieved of its tears—by the *living* weed. Similarly, the sailor who would give his eyes to possess the "indivisible" iceberg at last compromises and sails off on the human ship. Something "important" is being discovered in both poems (it's not very difficult to guess what), yet their images, their symbols, leave the reader with an ambivalent sense of significance. How strikingly different is the plain-speaking in one of Bishop's last poems, "Santarém." Here, as in "The Weed," she describes two rivers, this time wholly geographical South American rivers, the Tapajos and the Amazon, meeting at a center of trade and then "grandly, silently flowing, flowing east." After a bit of detailed description, the poet declares that she "liked the place. I liked the idea of the place."

> Two rivers. Hadn't two rivers sprung
> from the garden of Eden? No, that was four
> and they'd diverged. Here only two
> and coming together. Even if one were tempted
> to literary interpretations
> such as: life/death, right/wrong, male/female—
> such notions would have resolved, dissolved, straight off
> in that watery, dazzling dialectic.

How typical of Bishop! Any *dialectic* the place might suggest dissolves straight away in the details of an appearance. The reader is advised not to indulge in useless abstractions; ideas never do get anything right. Just look, just look. The rest of the poem is lightly descriptive, chatty, anecdotal. Though set out in lines with a justified left margin, it acts upon the imagination like prose. The poet supplies a brightly colored picture, say from the *National Geographic,* with an explanatory text attached. Especially noticeable is the way Bishop steers us away from any "meanings" we might be tempted to give the objects described, as if it were hopeless to try to identify meaning anyway. The place is enough. Full of *life,* shipping, people embarking, disembarking, rowing (not paddling) their "clumsy dories." There, now, is the cathedral, and a street deep in "dark-gold river sand"; and there are the usual palms, the usual stucco buildings painted blue and yellow. We learn, too, that after the Civil War a few Southern families emigrated to Santarém because there they could still own slaves. They bequeathed to the native people "occasional blue eyes, English names, / and *oars.*"

Elizabeth Bishop was especially fortunate in her gift for making everything she wrote interesting. Although she slaved over her poetry, she was a naturally prolific letter-writer—as everybody knows who has looked into the fat volume of her selected letters. If we choose, we can almost read "Santarém" as a letter, its tone is so consciously informal. And yet, give it a second and third reading, and doesn't something very like a "meaning" begin to emerge? Look at the last two stanzas:

> A week or so before
> there'd been a thunderstorm and the Cathedral'd
> been struck by lightning. One tower had
> a widening zigzag crack all the way down.
> It was a miracle. The priest's house right next door
> had been struck, too, and his brass bed
> (the only one in town) galvanized black.
> *Graçias a deus*—he'd been in Belém.
>
> In the blue pharmacy the pharmacist
> had hung an empty wasps' nest from a shelf:
> small, exquisite, clean matte white,
> and hard as stucco. I admired it
> so much he gave it to me.
> Then—my ship's whistle blew. I couldn't stay.
> Back on board, a fellow passenger, Mr. Swan,
> Dutch, the retiring head of Philips Electric,
> really a very nice old man,
> who wanted to see the Amazon before he died
> asked, "What's that ugly thing?"

As anyone who looks can see, the miracle in, or behind, this poem is *not* the priest's escape from incineration in his brass bed in his house next to the cathedral; it's the wasps' nest—the natural, not the religious miracle. Here is Elizabeth Bishop hinting again at a link with the Transcendentalists, but hinting so slyly that none but her most attentive readers will notice what she's up to.

I hope I have said enough to show that the difference between Bishop's poems and those of some latter-day imitators has to do with the nature of what is revealed through her surface descriptions. As she wrote early on in "The Weed," it's "As if a river should carry all / the scenes that it had once reflected / shut in its waters, and not floating / on momentary surfaces." Or, slyly again, in "Twelfth Morning; or What you Will": "Like a first coat of whitewash when it's wet, / the thin gray mist lets everything show through."

The difference, perhaps, between a major poet and a minor one has nothing to do with verbal exhibitionism or political righteousness or anything critically definable, but with an inner coherence that mysteriously unifies an entire oeuvre—and confirms it as "tremendously important" in the minds of a great many readers. Although Elizabeth Bishop's poems assume a variety of shapes, forms, and styles, and though it may be easy enough to trace her passage from "the dreamy state of mind" she said she lived in in her youth to the casual, intimate, very personal tone of her late work, her poems all point in the same direction.

Elizabeth Bishop was passionately fond of paintings—some, not all. She wrote of a Seurat in the New York Museum of Modern Art, "a smallish, quiet, gray & blue one of Honfleur, with posts sticking up out of the beach . . . I'd have given anything to have painted that!"[6] In the 1960s, she didn't at all approve of my comparing some of her descriptions to realistic paintings of rural America by Andrew Wyeth. (She was right about her tastes; she was a snob!) So I don't know what she would have made of the abstract expressionist paintings of another American, Jon Schueler, though I can't think she would have disapproved of this passage from his unpublished autobiography.

> The artist's search, his material, his hope, his failure cannot be defined. He is not concerned with definition, but with the illusion and elusiveness of reality itself. Indefinable. Untranslatable. It cannot be felt or seen, nor can its total image be burned upon our minds. Whoever looks knows that he sees so little that he, in effect, cannot see at all. By the very fact that, looking, he sees more than he has seen, he knows that he has not seen enough. Yet his only solution is to look more, to see more, to struggle to understand more.[7]

Elizabeth Bishop was surely all her life looking more and seeing more, but perhaps she decided fairly early on that struggling to understand more could be counterproductive. Intellectual struggles, abstract generalizations, all types of philosophizing except for the most simple tend to get in the way of seeing exactly what is given. In her poems, passages that superficially have little in common all share a quality of surprised revelation, of getting through to "what ever it is that one can never see full-face, but that seems enormously important." The Man-Moth who emerges from a sewer in the New York streets and swarms "up the facades / his shadow dragging like a photographer's cloth behind him" finds the sky "quite useless for protection" and takes to the subways. But there his escape through terrifying dreams is interrupted as, in effect, he is redeemed by the capture of his "one tear."

Tears. The source of life itself. Drops of water, each of which contains "a small, illuminated scene." The tears of St. Peter in "Roosters"—an antiwar poem in which the militaristic rooster is first transformed into a domestic weather vane on top of barns and steeples; and then into the craftsmen's little cock in church sculpture that mediates not only between Christ and his repentant disciple, but between ourselves and ourselves:

> yes, and there Peter's tears
> run down our chanticleer's
> sides and gem his spurs.
>
> . . . Poor Peter, heart-sick,
>
> still cannot guess
> those cock-a-doodles yet might bless,
> his dreadful rooster come to mean forgiveness,

Such tears prefigure those the almanac will plant in "Sestina." Tears also mutate into seeds in the fourth "Song for a Colored Singer," but there they appear to stand for something else, becoming the "black seeds" that root like dragon's teeth in the racist soil of Florida, promising the harvest of warriors.

> Fruit or flower? it is a face.
> Yes, a face.
> In that dark and dreary place
> each seed grows into a face.
>
> Like an army in a dream
> the faces seem,
> darker, darker, like a dream.
> They're too real to be a dream.

If tears, magical drops of water, bind Bishop's work together, so do a number of other images. Houses, for example—built, loved, wrecked, lost—are inevitably part of the lifelong sacrifice the sailors have to make to the iceberg. For in the end, of course, the iceberg has to win. No one escapes, for all the tears, trips, paintings, and lovely things of this world. And there are no safe houses, whether made of "chewed up paper / glued with spit" like Jeronimo's, or of imaginary bread, or of green shingles staked totteringly on a beach where a poet might retire and do nothing. The implication seems to be that we sailors ought to love and treasure (while we carefully observe) our earthly houseboat, together with its frail cargo ("clothes, crumbling postcards, broken china") before the inevitable wreck. Nowhere does Elizabeth Bishop suggest the possibility of an afterlife. She never once hints that transcendence occurs after death. The miracles she writes about all happen on earth.

In the end, it appears that nothing so crude as a split separates Elizabeth Bishop's earlier poetry from her later work. Perhaps the whole of it would be better described as an art form circling or flowing toward self-definition. Her poems became franker and clearer as they more and more risked sounding as simple as prose. It's as if, toward the end of her life, she felt she'd earned the right *not* to sound mysterious; the right to eschew artifice and say straight out what she meant. As it turns out, the more natural her poems look, the more mysterious her "message" seems to be. The strangest things in the world are, after all, always about us—in two senses, about us.

Writing, for instance, about a tiny painting of her Nova Scotia village "done in an hour" by her great-uncle (the one who painted the "Large Bad Picture" of her first book) she worked her writing brush steadily toward an epiphany so low-keyed that it pointedly rejects the word *vision*. Recognizing the scene of the painting, she meditates,

> Our visions coincided—"visions" is
> too serious a word—our look, two looks;
> art "copying from life" and life itself,
> life and the memory of it so compressed
> they've turned into one another. Which is which?
> Life and the memory of it so cramped,
> dim, on a piece of Bristol board,
> dim, but how live, how touching in detail
> —the little that we get for free,
> the little of our earthly trust. Not much.
> About the size of our abidance

along with theirs: the munching cows,
the iris, crisp and shivering, the water
still standing from spring freshets,
the yet-to-be-dismantled elms, the geese.

The Irish poet Eavan Boland has called Elizabeth Bishop "the one unromantic poet of her generation."[8] And when it comes to style and tone, these late poems certainly sound unromantic. They are not cleverly self-involved like John Berryman's; nor do they indulge in personal mythologies like some of Robert Lowell's. On the other hand, what could be more transcendent than that view of two artists' lives compressed in time? One is tempted to argue that little things in Bishop's poems are so intensely insisted on, looked at, looked into, that they do the visionary work of big ideas. She may have claimed for her poems only a Grade III rating as geographical guides to the world. Just the same, she had as much to say, I believe, as Wallace Stevens about "how to live and what to do."

Toward the end of her life, Bishop let her free verse flow almost all the way to prose. Who can prove that "Santarém," for example, is poetry, while "In the Village" is prose? Prose poems, poems' prose; the borderline is indistinct. Which is not to imply that Bishop ever ceased to take pains. Her object, as she herself often said, was to say complicated things as simply as possible— something she admired in George Herbert. For my taste, Bishop wrote at her best when she subjected her epistolary chattiness— that wonderful gift for witty personal intimacy—to formal restraint. Among the remarkable poems in *Geography III* are "One Art," which roughly obeys the rules for a villanelle, and "The Moose."

Consisting of twenty-eight irregularly rhymed stanzas, with six short lines each, "The Moose" was begun in 1946 (a letter to Marianne Moore describes the bus trip from Nova Scotia to Boston that set it going) but not completed until June 1972 when Bishop, working under pressure with encouragement from Frank Bidart, managed to finish it in time to read at the Phi Beta Kappa ceremony at Harvard. Twenty-six years to perfect twenty-eight stanzas—that must be something of a record!

The plot of "The Moose" is simple and, as we might expect, taken straight from experience. After visiting relatives in Great

Village, Nova Scotia, the speaker boards a bus traveling west and south through the red-earthed farming country at the head of the Bay of Fundy. She describes the long tides, the sequence of villages, the farms, the harbors in the simplest of language. In moonlight, the bus enters the New Brunswick woods as "the passengers lie back." Amid the "creakings and noises" a "dreamy divagation" begins: grandparents, great-grandparents, great-great-grandparents in the back of the bus are talking, finally settling up, tidying up a past that can only be overheard when the listener is half asleep. Such are this poet's intimations of Eternity. Yet how healing, how uncomplaining.

> "Yes . . ." that peculiar
> affirmative. "Yes . . ."
> A sharp, indrawn breath,
> half groan, half acceptance,
> that means "Life's like that.
> We know it (also death)."

At this point the poem seems to have reached, or earned, its meaning, which is as spiritual in its way as anything in Herbert or Wordsworth. Then suddenly the bus driver puts on his brakes.

> A moose has come out of
> the impenetrable wood
> and stands there, looms, rather,
> in the middle of the road.
> It approaches; it sniffs at
> the bus's hot hood.
>
> Towering, antlerless,
> high as a church,
> homely as a house
> (or, safe as houses).
> A man's voice assures us
> "Perfectly harmless . . ."

I suppose volumes could be written—probably are being written—to explicate this passage: the appearance of this huge, mild, ugly animal (not a bit like Yeats's great beast slouching toward Bethlehem), its femaleness, its churchlike size, its likeness to a house, and the irony of its being "safe as houses." The creature symbolizes anything and everything "otherworldly" in Bishop—though the moose is a creature of *this* world. So her academic critics are offered a veritable feast. But Bishop, as usual, wants nothing to do with meanings. Like the fish, the moose has its own meaning, and it quietly resists all clumsy linguistic efforts to tame it or reduce it to an idea. Can we say that the imaginary iceberg has been transformed in "The Moose" into a living animal, and that Bishop's ship full of artist-sailors has become, at a stroke of her wand, a battered bus full of half-awake ordinary people? Well, we might, perhaps. Even so, I doubt that Bishop would have liked to pursue such a "literary" analogy.

With "The Moose" Elizabeth Bishop's oeuvre comes full circle. Some epiphany or transcendence—showing through from behind a homely layer of whitewash, or, as here, through the mist and moonlight of the New Brunswick woods—is vouchsafed to the bus's passengers, who have been shaken awake as by a holy revelation. "Why do we feel," asks the poet, "why do we all feel this sweet / sensation of joy?" Why indeed? But before we can even begin to look for answers the bus driver shifts gears and drives on.

NOTES

1. Randall Jarrell, "Fifty Years of American Poetry," in *Third Book of Criticism* (New York: Farrar, Straus and Giroux, 1969), 325. See also Lloyd Schwartz and Sybil P. Estess, *Elizabeth Bishop and Her Art* (Ann Arbor: University of Michigan Press, 1983), 198.

2. Unpublished letter from Elizabeth Bishop to Anne Stevenson, December 30, 1963.

3. Letter to Anne Stevenson in *Elizabeth Bishop* (New York: Twayne, 1966), 66. See "The 'Darwin' Letter," in Schwartz and Estess, *Elizabeth Bishop*, 288.

4. Victoria Harrison, *Elizabeth Bishop's Poetics of Intimacy* (Cambridge: Cambridge University Press, 1993), 107–41.

5. Helen Vendler, "Domestication, Domesticity, and the Otherworldly," *World Literature Today,* winter 1977. Also Schwartz and Estess, *Elizabeth Bishop*, 32–48.

6. Unpublished letter from Elizabeth Bishop to Anne Stevenson, January 8–10, 1964.

7. Jon Schueler (1916–92), from the autobiographical manuscript "The Sound of Sleat."

8. Eavan Boland, "An Un-Romantic American," *Parnassus: Poetry in Review* 14, no. 2 (1966): 73–92. Quoted in Victoria Harrison, *Elizabeth Bishop's Poetics of Intimacy* (Cambridge: Cambridge University Press, 1993), 2.

II

Irish Issues

EAVAN BOLAND, NUALA NÍ DHOMHNAILL, SEAMUS HEANEY

The following two essays emerged in the course of a debate that took place during the early 1990s, chiefly in the pages of Poetry Nation Review *(PN Review), one of England's liveliest literary periodicals. The exchange began when, in response to an article by the Irish poet Eavan Boland, I sent the editors a lengthy critique, not of Boland's poetry, which I admire, but of the argument she had developed in her prose piece "Outside History." My article on Boland—"Inside and Outside History"—stirred up little interest in England, but in Ireland it enraged that ever-energetic spokeswoman for Irish women's poetry, Nuala Ní Dhomhnaill. Shortly thereafter, Ní Dhomhnaill published an attack on "Inside and Outside History" in* Poetry Ireland Review *(autumn 1992, 18–31), which, together with my reply, "Outside Histrionics," appeared again, the following spring, in* PN Review *(May–June 1993, 35–39).*

Both "Inside and Outside History" and "Outside Histrionics" are reprinted here with the permission of Michael Schmidt, editor of PN Review, *and I hope with the goodwill of the two Irish poets concerned. Nuala Ní Dhomhnaill, in the course of her attack, pointed out an egregious error in my text, and for this I am grateful to her. I have changed wording here and there in both pieces, noting but not deleting my mistake. The general drift of Boland's and Ní Dhomhnaill's papers should be clear from several quotations, but the full dispute makes interesting reading. See* PN Review *75 for Eavan Boland's article, 88 for mine, and 91 for Ní Dhomhnaill's and my exchange.*

Inside and Outside History

As will be evident to anyone who has followed Eavan Boland's purgatorial journey into self-placement, the story of her meeting with the Achill woman occurs at least twice in her published work: once in the verse sequence of *Outside History* (Carcanet, 1990), and again as a prologue to her essay of the same title (*PN Review,* 75). The story goes as follows: Boland, as a student at Trinity College, Dublin, had borrowed a friend's cottage on Achill Island for a week at Easter, bringing with her for study a volume of the court poets of the Silver Age, "those sixteenth century song-writers like Wyatt and Raleigh, whose lines appear so elegant . . . yet whose poems smell of the gallows." Since the cottage was without water, an old woman carried it up every evening in a bucket.

> I remember the cold rosiness of her hands.
> She bent down and blew on them like broth.
> And round her waist, on a white background,
> in coarse, woven letters, the words "glass cloth."
>
> And she was nearly finished for the day.
> And I was all talk, raw from college . . .

Both poem and essay mark the occasion as an epiphany, an incident that affected the direction of the poet's life and thinking. "She was the first person to talk to me about the famine. The first person, in fact, to speak to me with any force about the terrible parish of survival and death which the event had been in those regions." When the young poet turned her back on the woman and reentered the cottage to light a fire and memorize lines from the court poets, she was ignorantly turning, she says, away from her own history, away from the Achill woman and what she represented of Ireland's past in order "to commit to memory the songs and artifices of the very power system which had made [the old woman's] own memory such an archive of loss."

From *PN Review* 88 (1992). Reprinted with permission.

In her poetry, Eavan Boland raises the problem of her Irish identity in the context of that "archive of loss." At the same time, her concerns are much broader. Memory, change, loss, the irrecoverable past—such are the shared conditions of humankind with which she scrupulously engages. Her poems give an impression of a grave, even solemn intelligence, very little ruffled by the politics of nationalism, or, for that matter, by the women's movement. A sensitive poet, then, a woman unafraid of thought, rarely thrown off balance by anger; a poet willing to brave current fashions by freely advancing ideas—though she works, usually, with concrete images. Daringly, she calls a poem "We Are Human History. We Are Not Natural History," placing her children in the "short-lived" and "elegiac" light of a particular encounter with nature (a wild bees nest) so as to explore, in tentative yet exact language, her sense of our uniquely *human* experience of time and selective memory. "And this— / this I thought, is *how it will have been / chosen* from those summer evenings / which under the leaves of the poplars— / striped dun and ochre, simmering over / the stashed-up debris of old seasons— / a swarm of wild bees is making use of" (my italics).

Given the distinction Boland makes between human history and the natural world, one might expect an essay entitled "Outside History" to point to an area of release. Human history, seen as a record of power, struggle, war, and wastage, is indeed a horror story; the whole of it could be described as "a parish of survival and death." But to see *around* history into the filtering byways of individual creation and discovery can liberate the mind from useless self-laceration. I opened the essay "Outside History" with an expectation, founded on the poems, of engaging with a personal philosophy of survival. To my surprise, the essay, though very personal, turned out to be a polemic: a disquisition on the "virulence and necessity of the idea of a nation," and especially on how the poetic inheritance of Ireland has cut across the poet's identity as a woman.

Though Eavan Boland as an Irishwoman and I as an American are separated by very different historical experiences, her sympathy and fascination with the Achill woman is easy to share. The title "Outside History" points to that silent majority excluded from the history books whom the practitioners of "total history" have lately sought to bring inside history (as, for example, in Peter Laslett's *The World We Have Lost*). For most of us, probably, who seek to identify with the past but who feel excluded by gender or class or prejudice from the conventional national pasts of the history books, it is through these silent majorities that we must make our connections. Yet, is it only my American background that makes me pause before the "virulence and necessity of the idea of a nation"? For a Serbian or Croatian poet entering new nightmares after the long Ottoman centuries the language fits well enough. But for an Irish poet in a republic secure in the Economic Community, whose changing mood is now reflected in the election of a woman president? I'm not sure.

Historical perspective, perhaps, should also be brought to bear on Boland's central premise: "that over a relatively short time—certainly no more than a generation or so—women have moved from being the subjects and objects of Irish poems to being the authors of them." That almost all the Irish poets of *recent* periods have been male, and that in popular imagination women, by and large, have been little more than motifs for their love poems—yes, that no one could deny. Forget for a moment Yeats's complicated admiration for powerful political women: Maud Gonne, Constance Markowitz, Lady Gregory. Forget Joyce's warm, ebullient Molly Bloom (surely the character most likely to survive in *Ulysses*) and turn instead to the contents page of John Montague's *Faber Book of Irish Verse* (1978). Chronologically, after Thomas Moore (1779–1852) only two women's names appear: Eavan Boland herself, with one poem, and Eilean Ní Chuilleanain, with two. Today the list would be extended to include Maire Mhac an tSaoi, Nuala Ní Dhomhnaill, and Medbh McGuckian; perhaps one or two others. Still, that shows a tiny proportion of, say, six women to over sixty men. The anxieties, the bafflements, the evident distress Eavan Boland has experienced, given her contemporary social conscience and highly developed self-consciousness, look to be real enough.

I still recall my fury, one evening during the 1970s, after Montague himself, with James Simmons, had performed in the Old Fire Station, Oxford. Over drinks, insulted to be treated as an object of gallantry rather than a poet in my own right, I spoke rather hotly I believe to John Montague on the subject of women poets. Why could not (male) Irish poets take us seriously? Montague, to my surprise, laughed at my ignorance, maintaining that, on the contrary, women poets had never been discriminated against in Ireland. Many of the greatest poets in Irish had been women. I disbelieved him.

It was several years later that I came across a copy of *The Faber Book of Irish Verse* that John Montague must have been editing at the time. The introduction, dwelling on the oral tradition of early Irish literature, has first of all a good deal to say about the loss to Anglicized Irish poets of their national language. The rediscovery of ancient Irish literature was spurred on by the Celtic revival of Yeats's time, a movement that continues into the present. Most Irish poets, at some time in their lives, still exercise their talents by translating from medieval Irish epics. Heroic classics like *The Great Tain* and *Cuchulain* survived, ironically enough, in the monasteries. One paragraph in Montague's introduction struck me forcibly.

> And here we should remark another aspect of early Irish poetry: it is the only literature in Europe, and perhaps in the world, where one finds a succession of women poets. Psychologically, a female poet has always seemed an absurdity, because of the necessarily intense relationship between the poet and the Muse. [I doubt that Montague would risk such a chauvinist speculation today.] Why then did poetry always seem a natural mode of expression for gifted Irish women? I think this was because there was no discrimination against them; the first woman poet of whom we hear, Liadan of Corcaguiney, was a fully-qualified member of the poets' guild, which could mean as much as twelve years of study. It was as an equal that the poet Cuirithir wooed her, and though she drove him off, for religious reasons, her lament rings in our ears to this day.

A section of Montague's anthology is devoted to women and love in the ninth century—much of it love poetry written by women passionately to their men. The women's verse Montague represents in translation includes a famous prototype of Villon's "Belle Heaulmière" called "The Hag of Bere," Liadan's "Lament for Cuirithir," and, from the eighteenth century, Eibhlin Dubh O'Connell's "Lament for Art O'Leary"—the culmination, Montague says, of "a long line of such poems." Noticeable in all these poems by women is their frank sexuality, their energy, their wit, their piety—and particularly their lack of self-pity. Even as the Hag of Bere laments the loss of fortune, beauty, and love, she thanks God almost boastfully for departed glories.

> But I bless my King who gave—
> Balanced briefly on time's wave
> Largesse of speedy chariots
> And champion thoroughbreds.
>
> These arms, now bony, thin
> And useless to younger men,
> Once caressed with skill
> The limbs of princes!
>
> (Version: John Montague)

Do I hear faint feminist complaints that all these women were treated as sex objects whose verse only confirms that men have exploited women since history began? Without disagreeing, let's also remind ourselves that the past is indeed another country, and that when modern people pass judgment on long-dead societies they usually misrepresent them. Contemporary evidence reveals that women in the Irish sagas were greedily sexual, bawdy, humorous, vengeful when deceived or jealous, inconsolable in bereavement, but even in sorrow charged with an emotional energy uninhibited by Victorian prudishness and sentimentality or by individualistic twentieth-century self-consciousness. At a time when war, death, and love were poetry's chief subjects (mixed, in the Celtic tradition, charmingly with invocations to beasts, birds, and trees), it is delightful to realize that in sexual matters women asserted recognizable voices of their own. In Montague's version of "The Only Jealousy of Emer," for instance, the quarrel between Emer and Cuchulain gives a biting part to the woman.

> Emer: A question, fickle though you are,
> Cuchulain. Why did you shame me
> before all the women of Ulster,
> the women of Ireland, and
> all mannerly people?
> I came under your care,
> the full strength of your bond,
> and though success makes you vain,

it may be a while, little hound,
before you get rid of me.

Moving on to the thirteenth century, Giolla Brighde Mac-
Namee prays for a child. [I have since learned that Giolla Brighde
MacNamee was a male poet, but it seems best to retain the error
in view of Nuala Ní Dhomhnaill's riposte.]

> God I ask for two things only,
>   Heaven when my life is done,
> Payments as befits a poet—
>   For my poem pay a son.
>
> Plead with Him, O Mother Mary,
>   Let Him grant the child I crave,
> Womb that spun God's human tissue,
>   I no human issue leave.
>
> Brigid after whom they named me,
>   Beg a son for my reward,
> Let no poet empty-handed
>   Leave the dwelling of his lord.
>   (Version: Frank O'Connor)

What seems to be so moving about this plea is the poet's
domestic attitude toward religion. Begging two sainted women
to plead with God is like asking two virtuous daughters to inter-
cede with a stern father. Heaven is a family home in which
women are the approachable mediators. If, however, evidence
of blood-and-guts passion is desired, could a man write more
simply and forcefully than Dark Eileen, mourning for Art
O'Leary (1750?).

> I struck my hands together
> And I made the bay horse gallop
> As fast as I was able
> Till I found you dead before me
> Beside a little furze-bush.
> Without Pope or bishop,
> Without priest or cleric
> to read the death-psalms for you,
> But a spent old woman only
> Who spread her cloak to shroud you—

Your heart's blood was still flowing;
I did not stay to wipe it
But filled my hands and drank it . . .

(Version: Eilis Dillon)

I confess to being, at most, an enthusiastic amateur in Irish
studies. But surely, it is a point of fact that women of spirit and
gumption were not only roundly represented in the Gaelic tradi-
tion; they were writers in Irish themselves.* Eavan Boland inher-
its poetic authority from a long, healthy chain of foremothers.
Why hesitate to summon them, to translate them, to learn from
them? Why is her imagination not excited by these vivid figures
of the past but set off instead by the defeated image of the Achill
woman? Because, I think, the woman poets of the ancient Irish
tradition, bound as they were within tribal (sexual) conventions
and childlike Christian belief, have very little to offer her mod-
ern imagination. As a contemporary Western woman poet—and
she is that, perhaps, more than an Irish poet—Eavan Boland
craves confirmation from her peers; she asks them, those other
living Irish poets, for authority to write as an individual woman.
I have not noticed this confirmation to be lacking, but obviously
Eavan Boland feels—or has recently felt—that for women it is.

Seemingly something else is the matter, too. Perhaps it has to
do with what people, these days, expect poetry to be. Few would
deny that individuality, or what is termed an "original voice," is
judged to be of primary importance. At the same time, radical
ideologies—such as feminism—tend to predetermine the pub-
lic's (and the poet's) political point of view. How can a genu-
inely new individual voice speak with a communal tongue? How
can a poet honestly fulfill herself and at the same time meet the
requirements of pressure groups who want her to speak for
them? Perhaps this quandary is one source of Eavan Boland's
predicament.

For Eavan Boland, evidently, as once for Simone Weil, to
write of people "outside history" means, in effect, to find speech
to express the helpless suffering of thousands of undocumented

---

*Another famous woman poet of the eighteenth and nineteenth centu-
ries, not represented in Montague's selection but well known in the
Gaelic tradition, is Maire Bhui Ní Laoghaoire (1774–c. 1849).

78

forefathers and foremothers (such as the Achill woman) while burdening herself, too, with responsibility for contemporary torments. The ignorant and unfortunate will always be "outside history," *carent quia vate sacro,* unless poets commit themselves to telling their tales. All this, I should add, redounds very much to Eavan Boland's credit and says much for her responsive, empathetic heart. More questionable seems to be a doctrine that is also implicit in Boland's title. She seems to believe that male poets have excluded women from Irish history by systematically, in countless love poems and popular songs, transforming real women, with real sorrows, into mythical queens or magical Sibyls. Sentimental, symbolic Irish history, in her view, has "feminized the national and nationalized the feminine" until it is impossible for a woman to write in an authentic Irish voice.

By arguing that, on the contrary, Ireland inherits an ancient culture richly endowed with women poets, I am not contradicting Boland's claim to having been disadvantaged because of her gender; I am only suggesting that her discontent is of comparatively recent descent. As a contemporary complaint, it represents one aspect of a socially conscious, stoic yet historically misconceived poetic that today is overwhelmingly approved by a great many guilt-ridden and overprivileged Western intellectuals. Leaving aside the current crop of language-playing sophisticates, it is possible to see in Eavan Boland an almost typical fair-minded idealist who, morally and politically, would wish to contradict the elitist (and as she may see it, escapist) aesthetic that a group of Symbolists put forward a hundred years ago as the only hope for art in a barbarian age. I refer to the "beauty" paraded by Ruskin and Pater, the haughty exclusiveness of Mallarmé, even the romantic (not the later, skeptical) patriotism of Yeats.

Is it not, at heart, to that other fin de siècle's literary aesthetic—as well as to a tradition of popular Irish myth—that Eavan Boland takes exception? And doesn't such a socially focused poetic—I'm not attacking it—implicitly reject T. S. Eliot's passionate traditionalism, as also Wallace Stevens's insistence that poetry must above all be abstract? To Boland, it would seem, any notion of impersonal art, even of sacramental art, detached from moral responsibility *for individuals,* must be frivolous. It is significant that, while tossing out the myths of sentimental Ireland, Boland discards, too, the "English Poets of the Silver Age"—who, of course, knew nothing of a future in which "postmodernism" would morally condemn the "imperialism" that those Elizabethans saw as an expansion of the civilized, Christian world.

Probably such wholesale ideological rejections are healthy for poetry. History, as Yeats perceived, is a cyclical as well as a linear phenomenon. In every era poets define the history they shape and that shapes them. I trust that Eavan Boland is not suggesting in "Outside History" that her premises are final or absolute. She can, after all, speak only for herself and for the tiny crest of time upon which she rides. Meanwhile, she and women poets like her have brought to poetry a welcome compassion and appeal to moral consciousness.

At the same time, it is worth drawing attention to the selective picture such a viewpoint presents of actual history. During the reign of Elizabeth I, when the poets of the Silver Age were in full flower, a famous woman pirate and freebooter called Grainne Ní Mhaille (Grace O'Malley) beat off an English expedition against Carraig an Chabhlaigh castle, on the Mayo coast near Newport, south of Achill. That was in 1574. By 1580, after imprisonment in Limerick and Dublin, she was helping the English fight her own husband. Having survived two husbands and numerous arrests, Grainne at last appealed to Queen Elizabeth for "a license to harry the Queen's enemies with fire and sword" from Achill's shores. Her story has passed into the legends of that rocky and remote area (my information comes from *The Shell Guide to Ireland*) but its basis in truth again suggests that women in the Silver Age were not *always* the victims of "the very power system which had made [the Achill woman's] memory an archive of loss." Power is power, whether wielded by women or by men. Not only gender but opportunity, character, and class determine who beats up whom in history.

In the context of poetry, however, Eavan Boland's contribution is unquestionably valuable and valid. Nor would it be true to say that the deeply felt sociological wrongs she complains of in her essay in any way diminish the excellence of poems like "The Black Lace Fan My Mother Gave Me," "Object Lessons," and "Distances"—poems that seem to me as fine as any written in the past decade in the English language. Such reservations as I express, therefore, relate to Eavan Boland's framework of ideas, to her "dissociation of sensibility" if you like, and to the restrictions she places upon herself by self-consciously choosing a national/gendered role as a writer. Her very will to be "good"—in a humane sense—excludes, from some of her poems, some irrational, amoral, unpredictable fire or flair that the muse, without the slightest regard for social justice, occasionally lights in the hearts of the undeserving. Perhaps the muse herself resents being dismissed as a mere "myth." Look, for instance, at the way the title poem "Outside History" presents the poet in the act of lamenting an incorrect social attitude that has excluded thousands of sufferers from public memory.

The speaker, who in "Outside History" can be no one but Boland herself, begins, as she often does, by separating nature from history.

> There are outsiders, always. These stars—
> these iron inklings of an Irish January,
> whose light happened
>
> thousands of years before
> our pain did: they are, they have always been
> outside history.

Without questioning whether "iron inklings of an Irish January" accurately enough describes the universe, we can agree that history means the human story. And OK we accept this, even as we remind ourselves that history is contingent not upon the painful story of Ireland but upon the biological evolution of life through *millions* of years. Boland continues: "Under them [the stars] remains / a place where you found you were human, and / a landscape in which you know you are mortal." The references seem to be personal, and the poet appears to be addressing herself. It is impossible to tell, though, from the information given, whether the place in which she found she was human is identical with the landscape in which she knows she is mortal. The landscape is surely Ireland. Or Achill. The poem gives us to understand that a choice has to be made between two loyalties or affiliations, although the actual line "And a time to choose between them" is ambiguous. Between what? Between "a place where you found you were human" and "a landscape in which you know you are mortal?" No, it seems the choice she alludes to lies between escaping (like early Yeats) into Irish myth or accepting the appalling realities of Irish history. If the poet had imagined herself choosing between the stars, say, and the landscape of Ireland, then by choosing Ireland she would have chosen the ship (in Elizabeth Bishop's terms) over the iceberg. As it is, it may be that she has set up a false dichotomy. It is hard to understand why a poet feels bound to make a choice.

> I have chosen:
>
> out of myth into history I move to be
> part of that ordeal [Ireland's historical ordeal]
> whose darkness is
>
> only now reaching me from those fields,
> those rivers, those roads clotted as
> firmaments with the dead.

What the poem says, then, is that "I" (the poet) have at last chosen to move into the terrible history of Ireland's people. The darkness is "clotted as / firmaments with the dead" who are only now reaching her from *inside* history—just as light from the stars is reaching earth from outside history after journeying thousands of light-years in space. Having made her choice, the poet tries unavailingly to speak to and console the dead.

> How slowly they die
> as we kneel beside them, whisper in their ear.
> And we are too late. We are always too late.

Notice how the shifting pronouns show the poet as a leader of a group as the poem progresses from a "you" addressed at the beginning, to an "I" choosing the ordeal, to the "we" kneeling beside the dead in the last stanza. Boland has left the participants in that "we" to the reader's imagination. I myself read it, in the light of Boland's other work, as referring to Irish women poets, but it could refer, too, simply to Irish poets or to sympathetic people in general.

That the poem is well made and heartfelt is not in question. What worries me chiefly is a feeling, or half a feeling, of being present at the creation, not of a new approach to history but of a new myth. Look at what actually happens when, from a comfortable niche in middle-class modern Ireland, a woman poet looks back at the horrors of the past and *decides* to choose history over myth. Not being able really to enter history, she instead creates a highly imaginative scene—"roads clotted as / firmaments with the dead"—in which she and other poets participate as a chorus of mourners.

Now, does not such a poetic tragedy as Boland creates partake more of myth than of history? It seems to me that there is no way a poet can choose history and reject myth without giving up poetry altogether and taking instead to medicine or social work, or martyrdom. The very making of a poem—especially one in which the poet acts the leading role—ensures that the past is reshaped and fictionalized. It seems more honest to admit that a poet can do nothing with history but make poetry from it. And that's a wonderful thing to be able to do! The finest poetry, as Seamus Heaney has famously argued, *redresses* history by raising it up, encoding it in song and story. Compare the hand-wringing pathos of Boland's evocation of history's dead with Eibhlin Dubh O'Connell's vigorous endorsement of life at the end of her lament for Art O'Leary.

> My love and my treasure,
> Your stacks are roped,
> Your cows heavy with milk
> But sorrow in my heart
> All Munster can't cure,
> Nor the druids of the past.
> Until Art O'Leary comes again.
> This sorrow won't lift
> That lies across my heart
> Like a tightly-locked trunk
> With rust on the hasps
> And the key thrown away.
>
> So stop your weeping now
> Women of the soft, wet eyes
> And drink to Art O'Leary
> Before he enters the grave school
> Not to study wisdom and song
> But to carry earth and stone.
>
> (Version: John Montague)

Part of the attraction of Irish literature is its enduring robustness. Irish women poets of the present need look no further back than to the eighteenth century and that amazing harangue flamboyantly voiced in Brian Merriman's comic dream sequence "The Midnight Court." In the course of this mock-epic, which is nothing if not feminist in theme and tone, the poet— together with all the drab, unwedded, sexually lazy men of Ireland (including clerics)—is roundly indicted by a court composed of frustrated women intent on avenging themselves for sexual neglect. The whole poem is, in fact, a dazzling send-up of exactly the sentimental feminization of Ireland that Eavan Boland complains about in her essay. And still, the most effective form of literary complaint is mockery, satire.

Women of Ireland, make fun out of your fury! Deliver your judgments on male pompousness with a flickering tongue! The precedents are there throughout the Celtic tradition. Only contemporary self-consciousness and a socially sanctioned piety far more inhibiting than old-fashioned Irish religion could snuff out the truly pagan spirit of the Irish past by substituting ideology for mythology and hand-wringing for energy and wit.

Outside Histrionics
Answering Nuala Ní Dhomhnaill

Since I am accused by Nuala Ní Dhomhnaill of "a subtle sneering tone that pervades [my] whole piece" on Eavan Boland's "Outside History," I should first reiterate my expressed regard for Eavan Boland's poems, "which seem to me as fine as any written in the past decade in the English language." "She and woman poets like her," I wrote, "have brought to poetry a welcome compassion and an appeal to moral consciousness. . . . Eavan Boland is an exemplary poet of her time." "Such reservations as I express," I went on, "relate to Eavan Boland's framework of ideas, to her 'dissociation of sensibility' if you like, and to the restrictions she places upon herself by self-consciously choosing a national/gendered role as a writer." That is not what I call berating her. It is for stumbling into charged areas of nationalism and sexism that I have myself been berated and found guilty, without extenuating circumstance, of the grave political offense of obscurantism.

My suggestion that "Eavan Boland as an Irishwoman and I as an American are separated by very different historical experiences" triggered some shrill rhetoric on the tragedy of the Amerindians. The point, not a new one, has often and rightly been made by hostile critics. Fanny Trollope, for example, appalled by the casual manners and lack of deference in white America, was quick to point to the irony of the new democracy's ill treatment of black people and Indians. For another continent, Robert Hughes, in *The Fatal Shore,* told the terrible story of Australia's indigenous inhabitants who over many millennia had adapted their lives to the constraints of a difficult environment, only, within the last two centuries, to be exterminated or demoralized by victims of social punishment from the other side of the world. It's a story, isn't it, that in one form or another has been told throughout history? And our consciousness of colonialism today, as of pollution, overpopulation, and environmental exploita-

From *PN Review* 91 (1993). Reprinted with permission.

tion, is international; a burden of guilt we share across national boundaries: the horizontal (so to speak) of a cross whose vertical is our own personal, local, or national history.

"Coming from America," I am told, "where the chthonian aboriginal earth energies have been more or less wiped out . . . [I] can have no hint of a tint of a clue of what it is like to live in a country such as Ireland." Lucky Nuala, then, who finds it "infinitely more exciting and much more of a human challenge to live in a country which is even . . . intermittently in touch with the irrational than in one which has set its face resolutely against it." But these wild generalizations conceal—and this is my quarrel with them—a great deal of common ground. While suspicious of phrases like "chthonian earth energies," I am happy to have a confirmation of my own sense of Ireland. To live there should be a cause for rejoicing (despite the pope and the bombs), not for moaning about being colonized! Is it a worse fate to live in a country that was colonized than in one (look at post-Thatcher England) that was once a colonial power?

Similarly, Ní Dhomhnaill's delineation of the differences between a rational and a "psycho-emotional-imagistic dimension of being" conceals an area of common experience under its rhetoric. That "a whole realm of powerful images exists within us, overlooked by, and cut off from, rational consciousness" is not a statement I would ever dispute. I cannot take seriously, though, the implication that such a state of mind is inaccessible to someone brought up in America. Can't we please get away from hollow psychospeak, remote from the complexities of reality, as from a self-righteous extremism misused to divide and separate where really there is much in common? Behold, the mind-forged manacles, at it again!

The question remains, still, why did I write that piece in response to Eavan Boland's "Outside History." Why did her article get under my skin? Because, I think, both nationalism and women have become cults in today's world, and where there are cults there are bound to be stereotypes. And where there are stereotypes, false language soon drives out the specifics of perception. (One sees this happening on nearly every page, for instance, of Edward Said's *Culture and Imperialism*.)

For Nuala Ní Dhomhnaill, as for Eavan Boland, the romantic stereotype of Ireland as a noble woman (or as Mother Ireland) constitutes, it seems, a terrible threat to today's real Irish women, particularly Irish women poets. Why? The image evolved over hundreds of years, during which time an idealized woman—a figure of popular imagination comparable to the Virgin—provided an understandable mythical alternative to the reality of oppression and defeat. Today such a symbol is no longer so relevant. I wrote in response to Eavan Boland's article to remind her, as well as myself, that women in Ireland and Gaelic Scotland had inherited a long history of making and chanting poetry. Having consulted John Montague's *Faber Book of Irish Verse* and looked again at Daniel Corkery's classic study, *The Hidden Ireland,* which gives quite a lot of space to the "keen," I concluded that in Ireland women, rather surprisingly, had never been consciously excluded from Celtic culture, and that in their own verse as in much poetry written by men, they frequently appeared as their energetic, formidable, and very witty selves.

Nuala Ní Dhomhnaill, in the course of delivering a flyting worthy of the fiercest of her foremothers, mocks me for making mistakes. Indeed, others have chided me more gently for wrongly surmising that Giolla Brighde MacNamee must have been a woman. I apologize for this clear manifestation of ignorance. Yet I don't see that one mistake spoils my thesis. Ní Dhomhnaill herself insists that "hundreds, even thousands of women" were skilled in the art of the lament. Surely the precedent is there. Already, she says, the "canon" is being modified by Irish women scholars, while Caitlin Maude and Maire Mhac an tSaoi happily have provided her with "role models." So what is Nuala's problem? As a poet writing in Irish (whether because she has "no choice" or whether, as she also claims, it is "the main post-colonial strategy we use") she has this to say about her position.

Women poets in Irish were always highly discriminated against, and still are. . . . When I first experimented with the long line it was deemed unprintable. . . . You name it, I've suffered it; the lack of freedom, the lack of adequate critical reaction, the lack of reviews. . . . It has been a long and tedious struggle for us women writing in Irish to get even a precarious toehold in visibility. . . . The two concepts of "women" and "poet" seem incapable of being entertained simultaneously by the tiny little minds of the literati of this island.

This cry from the heart lends quite a seductive appeal to the call for gender solidarity in the face of gender oppression. Its objectivity is hard to assess from the other side of the Irish Sea, but one does wonder. "Lack of adequate critical reaction"? A commonplace refrain of poets of either sex. And is life that easy for "male poets" writing in Irish? How printable would the long line have been had a man written it? Isn't the problem of modernizing a traditional canon common to Gaelic and Welsh, whichever the poet's gender? Literary establishments are generally pernicious (not least feminist ones), but one thing is for sure: where there are male establishments, they will be only too happy to be handed on a plate the category of women poets. This complicitous consignment to the ghetto is perhaps the worst burden that poets who are women have to endure.

I can see that for Eavan Boland, who writes in English, "role models" in Irish (if one needs such things) may not offer much support. Born of an Irish family but brought up, if I am not mistaken, in London, she studied poetry at Iowa and publishes in the *New Yorker*. A huge "women's support group" is available to her in the States, and increasingly women poets are beginning to make names for themselves in England, Scotland, and Wales. Apparently it is only in Ireland that she feels neglected. But why should Boland let the fact that she is a woman and Irish bother her so much? Is it somehow the fault of "male poets" as fine as Montague, Heaney, Mahon, Longley, and Muldoon that she feels herself to be an outsider? Or could it be that the old stereotype nationalism offers her (Mother Ireland) and the new stereotype the women's movement has conjured up (Woman Poet) are in conflict? I rather think this to be the case, although to suggest that the category "woman poet" is no more than a stereotype is, of course, to invite censure.

Nevertheless, it seems to me important that some women question the necessity of there being "women poets" of a species different from "men poets." I do not lose sleep because Shakespeare was a man. (Did Sappho agonize over the lack of women poets on Lesbos?) Nor do I lie awake worrying about whether I am an American or an English woman, or asking myself whether, as either, I have a right to live and write in Wales. Such matters, consciously brought to mind by the culture we live in, are extraneous to poetry. For poetry, as Nuala Ní Dhomhnaill knows very well, is not based on role models or cultural visibility or "post-colonial strategy" but is indeed, as she says, "a delineation of the human soul, and the human soul is a fuming abyss. Sarajevo is just down the road." Exactly.

So Nuala Ní Dhomhnaill and I agree on many points. I would even suggest that with Eavan Boland and Marina Warner, we are at heart much the same kind of feminist. I most resolutely reject, however, all jargon that attempts to relegate poetry to matters of political or personal expediency. A great amount of poetry in all cultures has been written by men in praise of women. But if women have been adored, worshiped, idealized in the past, does that really inhibit their drive to express themselves now? Nuala Ní Dhomhnaill cites statistics to prove it does, but frankly I don't trust statistics collected under pressure of suggestion. In the eighteenth century one would have found statistical support among French women for the psychological theories of Franz Mesmer; in the nineteenth, the "science" of phrenology was taken seriously by women as astute as George Eliot. Every age has its intellectual illusions. The only way I know to insure poetry against the misconceptions and stereotypes of our time is to distrust all cultural generalizers and, as a woman or man, allow oneself to make poetry out of the particular. That will be the poetry that lasts and that eventually will represent the imagination and culture (whatever its faults) of our period.

The Peace within Understanding

Looking at Seamus Heaney's Preoccupations

In an early essay entitled "The Perfect Critic," T. S. Eliot was at pains to distinguish the practice of criticism from the practice of poetry. Though it is likely, he said, that the poet and the critic will be the same person (since "superior sensibility" is "rare, unpopular and desirable"), nevertheless, "the two directions of sensibility are complementary" but distinct. The perfect critic, according to Eliot, must avoid two extremes: overintellectualization on one hand—because it apes scientific organization—and impressionistic aestheticism on the other. In the early years of this century, critics tended to the latter extreme, and it was primarily at the aesthetic successors of Walter Pater that Eliot directed the admonitions of the first part of his essay. But in recent years twentieth-century critics have leaned in the other direction; so it was with foresight that in part 2 of "The Perfect Critic" Eliot turned his attention to the misuse of emotional and linguistic systematization.

One wonders at this stage what Eliot would have made of Seamus Heaney's *Preoccupations,* which seems to fall into a category Eliot did not anticipate. Heaney's essays are hardly impressionistic in the way Arthur Symons's were. They do not exclaim ecstatically over characters and plots or deliver opinions with regard to the meaning of poetic masterpieces. And yet, all the essays in *Preoccupations* are conspicuously personal. They fall so far short of contemporary standards of "emotional systemization" that we read them as we do Heaney's poems, as distinctive perceptions of a humane intelligence and an eminently generous personality.

It may be that Heaney himself does not consider some of the essays in this book to be "criticism." The memoirs that begin the collection and the moving tribute to Robert Lowell that ends it are personal in the way Heaney's poems are personal—

From *Symposium on the Poetry of Seamus Heaney,* ed. Tony Curtis (Bridgend, Wales: Seren Books, 1980). Reprinted with permission.

lucid and meticulously fair. Nevertheless, to Eliot, *Preoccupations* might just have verged upon the self-indulgent, since Eliot himself was, as he approvingly wrote of Swinburne, "one man in his poetry and a different man in his criticism." The intellectual and spiritual strains in Eliot's work proceeded in parallel but distinct lines; indeed, the very stiffness and dryness of his prose seemed to give impetus to the powerful religious intensity of his verse.

We can see right away that Heaney is a poet of an entirely different order, that his poetry and prose are branches of the same tree. The more we read of him, the clearer it becomes how deeply the root of that tree is embedded in the Irish soil of Heaney's childhood. At the same time, neither his poetry nor prose appear to be self-indulgent in the way, for instance, Eliot thought Arthur Symons was. Even Eliot would have agreed, I think, that Heaney's personal impressions rarely make concessions to sentimentality.

Heaney's gift for loving but distanced reminiscence is enhanced by two prevailing preoccupations (the book is well named), one of which it is certain Eliot would have approved. This is Heaney's fascination with language—his imagination that Eliot would have termed "auditory." In his essay on Hughes, Hill, and Larkin called "Englands of the Mind," Heaney uses Eliot's formulation as a touchstone for his own perceptions. But in Heaney (as in Eliot) "auditory imagination" is not only critical terminology; it is a mainspring of his own inspiration. He sees his contemporaries as "living off the hump of English poetic achievement," as he himself draws from the "word-hoard" of the past. What Heaney says about the language of these poets is incisive and true; but by putting their language first, before their meanings or their subject matters, Heaney achieves that distinctively inside perspective on their poetry that a purely academic critic might miss.

The other way in which Heaney eases the burden of his personality has to do with his concern for the emotional and spiritual state of Ireland, and of course, by example of Ireland, for the world itself. Heaney has been criticized—sometimes it seems that he criticizes himself—for not taking sides in the Troubles, for refusing to put a poetic shoulder to the wheel of Irish national sentiment, but instead, opting (more dangerously) for neutrality—as Dante did during the factional fighting in thirteenth- and fourteenth-century Italy.

Like Dante, Heaney declares an affinity only to peace. Whatever private answers he has made to political criticism, Heaney's considered explanation of his attitude appears consistently and constantly, both in his poetry and in his prose. It is as if it were being more and more fiercely borne in on him just how important peace is to his view of life and of art. In his poems, Heaney writes of peace as Keats—and Wallace Stevens—wrote of beauty, as a state of mind indispensable to creation. The first paragraph of *Preoccupations* is a quotation by way of an epigraph from Yeats's *Explorations* in which Yeats, in turn, quotes from Coventry Patmore: "The end of art is peace." The same inherited quotation appears as a climax in the last verse of "The Harvest Bow"— among the strongest and most personal poems in *Field Work*.

If, then, we see peace as a condition germane to Heaney's art, and we read his poems and essays in the light of this, we can see how Heaney's sensibility as an artist differs from Eliot's sixty years ago. Heaney's commitment to the art of poetry is no less passionate than Eliot's, but Heaney's is essentially a secular commitment, both in the manner of its language and in its fundamental subjectivity. As Heaney himself declared (after Yeats) in an excellent piece of self-analysis written for the *Guardian* in 1972 (*Preoccupations*, 34),

> You have to be true to your own sensibility, for faking of feelings is a sin against the imagination. Poetry is out of the quarrel with ourselves and the quarrel with others is rhetoric.

Here, of course, is a case of *Eriger en lois ses impressions personnelles*. For it cannot be said truly that *all* poetry is out of the quarrel with ourselves, only that the kind of poetry Heaney writes is. Heaney's personality and self-conflicts are so central to his perceptions that the abstracting quality Eliot valued (and with equal frankness tended to erect into laws) is sometimes hidden.

This is not to say that either Eliot or Heaney is "right" in what he claims for art and poetry, but only that they work (or worked) from different principles. In all his criticism and verse, distinguished as it is, Eliot deliberately retreats from himself. He grants us no confidences or personal memoirs. The personal pronoun *I* is never a focus for the ideas and feelings he presents—although certainly these ideas and feelings have a source in one person's committed, even prejudiced, point of view. Eliot's poetry primarily relates to his preoccupation with language in search of faith; his criticism relates to language in search of objectivity in the discussion of poetry. His strengths, both as a poet and a critic, derive from the objectifying austerity of his intelligence, which enabled him to abstract and universalize his feelings without reference to his autobiography. His method was more like that of the Milton he attempted to downgrade than of the Dante he revered.

On a first impression, it looks as if Heaney is closer to Dante in temperament than Eliot was, though of course Heaney is not prone to rehearse the theology of his day in his poems (for theology, substitute science, and we see that Heaney is very different in this respect); nor has Heaney so far engaged in the satisfying activity of populating Hell with his enemies. Heaney's affinity with Dante, as we might expect, is different from Eliot's. It is Dante's personal predicament that attracts him—Dante's situation in his society (similar to his own) as a scholarly, imaginatively just man who adheres to peace in an environment corrupted by politics and rife with murderous betrayal.

Since Dante is a greater poet—or at least a greater influence in poetry—than any writer of the twentieth century, it is not surprising that Eliot and Heaney have taken from *The Divine Comedy* what respectively they needed to nourish their very different sensibilities. Eliot interpreted Dante's poem as a religious one; Heaney looks to Dante's humanity and sense of justice in the light of his craving for peace. But presumably both poets, in the first instance, responded with excitement to the beauty of Dante's language, and both knew how vital their sense of Dante's art was to their own.

This pillaging of literary precedent is in accordance with Eliot's famous pronouncement with regard to tradition and individual talent; and it also illuminates Heaney's private admission in *Preoccupations* that "the feminine element for me involves the matter of Ireland, and the masculine strain is drawn from the involvement with English literature."

This is a particularly interesting admission, for it is precisely the "feminine" element that is absent from Eliot's criticism. If

Heaney's *Preoccupations* represents an advance on the critical dichotomy Eliot so carefully set up and analyzed in "The Perfect Critic," then Heaney's personal reconciliation between the feminine and masculine sides of his nature is not self-indulgence but a kind of intellectual discovery. It relates closely to the concept we have of intelligence. For if we conceive of intelligence as something distinct from emotion, as Eliot did—if we think of bringing *in* intelligence, as it were, like a schoolmaster to settle a fight between rowdy children, then we miss the subtlety of what intelligences like Heaney's have to teach us. Because Heaney is able to marry intelligence with personal feelings, he is able to bring to these essays a wisdom, an understanding that we all recognize but rarely feel free to express.

When subject becomes object (as it often does in Heaney's prose) or rather, when that synthesis occurs between subject and object which, familiar to us in poetry, seems somehow forbidden to us in criticism, we automatically fall into the type of thinking of which Eliot's is an example. We separate off and downgrade our emotions (feminine) by "handling" them with our minds (masculine). I must hastily add that women as well as men habitually adopt a "masculine" attitude in argument. What I am getting at has nothing to do with what sex we are, but everything to do with what we might call a prejudiced sexualization of ideas over feelings.

It is by overcoming this prejudice, by marrying and balancing intelligence and feeling, that Heaney achieves that warm yet rigorous empathy which enables him—as no other critic I know—to enter into the creative minds of the poets he considers. Naturally, Heaney writes most intimately of poets whose imaginations accord with his own—of Wordsworth, whose voice emerged out of a music overheard in nature and in childhood, and of Patrick Kavanagh, in whom Heaney finds the spiritual father he does not find, really, in Yeats. It is hard to imagine more sympathetic criticism of either of these poets. Yet in both "The Makings of a Music," which contrasts the speaking voices of Wordsworth and Yeats, and in "The Sense of Place," in which an illiterate, unconscious (feminine) sense of place is seen, in Kavanagh, to coexist with a determined (masculine) literary consciousness, Heaney proceeds from questions in his own mind that are central to his personal creative needs.

For all his Irishness, what Heaney seems to be doing in *Preoccupations* is exploring in prose the vein opened up by Robert Lowell in *Life Studies*. After *Life Studies* it seemed possible (perhaps it always was) to break with Eliot, with impersonality, with the stern patriarchal injunction to reduce the female-infected ego—at least in criticism—to invisible pulp. Lowell, under the influence of his psychoanalysis, reestablished himself and his life as significant material with which to build, not only a poetry but a literature. Heaney, instinctively breaking the rules banning autobiography and "self-indulgence," nevertheless understands the advantages of detachment (as Eliot would have understood that term). Rather than shutting out or abandoning the masculine mode of criticism, Heaney brings to it his natural feeling for mystery and divination . . . a femaleness that enriches his poetry to an extent not yet realized, possibly, by the more extreme protagonists of the feminist movement.

Nowhere is the strength of Heaney's androgynous understanding more apparent than in his essay on Gerard Manley Hopkins. Heaney takes as his text the "fire i' the flint" passage from *Timon of Athens:*

> Our poesy is as a gum which oozes
> From whence 'tis nourished: the fire i' the flint
> Shows not till it be struck; our gentle flame
> Provokes itself, and, like the current, flies
> Each bound it chafes.

Predictably, Heaney finds in this passage a parallel between the "gum that oozes" and that "word-hoard" of the embryonic but auditory imagination from which he draws so richly in his poetry. But Heaney is here not so much concerned to explore this home ground of poetic psychology (although he quotes from Eliot, Valéry, Blake, and Keats to show the extent of it) as he is to show how Hopkins develops his art out of the other half of Shakespeare's definition. It is from flint that Hopkins strikes his fire, and in contrast to the "oozy marshlight" of symbolism, Hopkins's "fretted" and "patterned" masterpieces exude a masculine brilliance, a command of language that disciplines passion and brings about a music of "deliberating intelligence." Poetry to Keats, says Heaney, has a physical equivalent in the birth pangs of a mother. But Hopkins brings to his craft a siring instinct. "Keats has the life of a swarm, fluent and merged; Hopkins has the design of the honeycomb, definite and loaded. In Keats, the rhythm is narcotic, in Hopkins it is a stimulant to the mind. Keats woos us to receive, Hopkins alerts us to perceive."

Now this is all most enlightening and informative. Heaney's analysis of Hopkins draws on that part of his imagination which gives itself, fluidly and generously, to another poet's reality. Heaney could never have written "The Wreck of the Deutschland," but he nevertheless sees that it is Hopkins's whole "myth"—a myth, moreover, that "has been lived as the truth by generations before and since Hopkins"—which was lived, too, by Dante and T. S. Eliot, but not, seemingly, by Heaney himself. It is all the more remarkable, therefore, that Heaney so perfectly realizes the "congruence" Hopkins's poetry builds between that poet and his faith, that he sees so clearly that "state of negotiation" (as Ted Hughes has put it) "between the man and his idea of a Creator" without which Hopkins's poetry would never have come into being.

So perhaps the outstanding impression left by this essay, as by most of *Preoccupations,* is of a wise man's liberality that, though personal, is perfectly unselfish. The integrity Heaney brings to his insights is more remarkable (and this is saying a great deal) than the insights themselves. In *Preoccupations* we are given a rare opportunity to explore the creating mind of a brilliant poet who would prefer to let us into the workings of his imagination than to keep us suspiciously at a distance. Heaney's openness is at times frightening; we almost fear for him, for he seems to have no defenses—not even a faith.

But perhaps the wise innocence of his penetrating intelligence *is* a sort of faith. As we have seen, Heaney's imagination has been able to draw strength equally from the "hump" of the English literary tradition and from the fecund "bog" of his own and Ireland's history. Out of these conscious and unconscious hemispheres of experience he has constructed a habitable inner world that we may call understanding. The peace Heaney makes for us and himself lies within understanding, even if it may be unachievable in the world outside it. And as for the peace that *passeth* understanding—well that is something Heaney seems, as yet, unprepared to define: Eliot's "still point of the turning world" . . . Dante's "L'Amour che move il sole e l'altre stelle."

Stations

Seamus Heaney and the Sacred Sense
of the Sensitive Self

As long ago as 1975, Frank Ormsby's *Ulster Publications* brought
out a sequence of twenty-one prose poems by Seamus Heaney
called *Stations*. In a short introduction Heaney described the
genesis of these pieces—a genesis that began in California in
1970–71 but that "rapidly came to a head" in 1974, a month
after the introduction of internment in Belfast. What began,
then, as a series of psychoautobiographical sketches, "attempts
to touch what Wordsworth called 'spots of time,' moments at the
very edge of consciousness," was delayed by the appearance of
Geoffrey Hill's *Mercian Hymns* ("What I had regarded as stolen
marches in a form new to me had been headed off by a work of
complete authority") but partly, too, by the hesitations of
Heaney's political conscience. Returning to Belfast from Amer-
ica, Heaney discovered that his "introspection was not confident
enough to pursue its direction."

If "direction" here means pursuit of the psychological sources
of Heaney's poetry—the searching out of private epiphanies
lost in the all but unconscious memories of childhood—then
Stations is as clear a declaration as we have of Heaney's di-
lemma as a post-Romantic, post-Freudian poet confronted by
an impersonal, probably insoluble, national crisis. Let's ignore
Heaney's Irishness for the present and look instead at his
Romanticism. I assume we can agree without prejudice that
Heaney (like Lowell, whom lately he begins to resemble) could
not and would not have written quite as he has, had it not been
for the example of Wordsworth (and only *after* Wordsworth,
Yeats, Joyce, and Patrick Kavanagh). For in Wordsworth we
have the first instance in Britain of a poet in retreat from a
corrupting society and a doubtful religion, digging in and forti-

From *Symposium on the Poetry of Seamus Heaney*, ed. Tony Curtis (Bridg-
end, Wales: Seren Books, 1980). Reprinted with permission.

fying the bastions of his own psyche. The poet as hero appears Romantically, of course, in Goethe and in Byron; yet it is in Wordsworth that his *retreat* is most in evidence, his withdrawal from the world into a sacred area of personal sensitivity; opposing to the world not only nature (this was a practice older than Shakespeare, older than Virgil) but, *in* nature, a subjective, unrational self.

It would be simpleminded, indeed silly, to claim—as some critics have claimed—that this sacred sense of the self that is Heaney's well-spring of imagination is mere self-indulgence. For who is to say with certainty that a single poet's experience is, in fact, singular? Whitman's *Song of Myself* extended that "self" into a kind of broadcasting device for the promulgation of ecstatic love. Wordsworth's more particular "self" found in childhood and nature a solace for frustrated revolutionary idealism. So each, in different ways, spoke for his age, or for the questing, Romantic spirit of that age.

In Heaney's case, though he speaks for *his* age, we perceive a difference. Political and philosophical idealisms no longer have the hold over our imaginations that they did during the nineteenth century. Nor are our notions of what is possible in human society as confident or as exuberant as those of pre-Freudian, pre-Jungian, pre-Nazi, or even pre-Vietnam Romantics. We are all of us sufferers from failure, a failure not so much of religion in any formal sense, but of Romanticism itself and the freedom to love and suffer that Romanticism, explicitly or implicitly, promoted as a dominant faith. Heaney, with his Wordsworthian instincts and gifts, has come to fame within a framework of doubt that, as in the case of Robert Lowell, is easily converted into guilt. In pursuit of nourishment for art, poets like Heaney are confronted with public pressure (a pressure they possibly imagine to be stronger than it is) to *do* something about a public situation. As an Irish Catholic in Ulster, Heaney should have something to say (such, I imagine, has been his own feeling). And in *North,* of course, he did find something to say; but that something did not quite answer the abiding and gnawing question of what, also, to *do.*

Understanding Heaney had, and still has, in abundance, and yet he casts "the stones of silence":

I who have stood dumb
when your betraying sisters,
cauled in tar,
wept by the railings,

who would connive
in civilized outrage
yet understand the exact
and tribal, intimate revenge.

North appeared in the same year as *Stations*—1975; so it would
seem that in the poems of this period (written in the first half of
the 1970s) Heaney imaginatively came to an understanding of
his position through an exploration of a particular history and
society. As nature was for Wordsworth, the Bog People were for
Heaney. Through them and their sacrifices Heaney reconciled
himself, however painfully, to privately understanding "the ex-
act, tribal" nature of the IRA's revenge. At the end of *North,* that
most revealing of poems, "Exposure," shows us Heaney's self as
antihero full of "responsible tristia," but for what?

I am neither internee nor informer;
An inner émigré, grown long-haired
And thoughtful; a wood-kerne

Escaped from the massacre,
Taking protective colouring
From bole and bark.

Responsible for himself, then. In the exquisite poems of *North*
Heaney is retreating into an area of personal sensitivity, just as
Wordsworth did. But instead of looking outward from his hole
into

Ye Presence of Nature in the sky
And on the earth! Ye Visions of the hills!
And Souls of lonely places!

Heaney is compelled instead to look inward and backward, into
himself and backward into history, into the human bog. No
wonder he feels he has missed "The once-in-a-lifetime portent, /
The comet's pulsing rose."

In coming to—or digging himself into—this position in *North,* Heaney made some of his best poems—poems that paradoxically speak publicly of his failure, and out of this failure, reach successfully to a huge, not necessarily Irish audience. What he shares with his readers is not the Irish question, nor is it his personal grief (although that is there). No. What he shares, or manifests, is precisely failure itself—that "failure" which in our time has become a hallmark of honesty, that "confession" which, in the work of Sylvia Plath, John Berryman, and Robert Lowell has cleared the air of false ideals, "Visions," "Presences," and mysticism itself. And if the strengths of the mode of confession—of failure—are such as to appeal to many of us, especially Americans, why should poets worry about what to do or say about particular political situations—such as now in Ireland? Why not go on confessing failure in the face of human unredeemability . . . confessing it very beautifully, as Heaney and Hill do?

Stations, I think, provides us with a hint of an answer to this question. For *Stations* is not a book of poems, as *North* is, but a collection of highly charged prose pieces that Heaney asks to do the work of poems. And this, for all their skill with words, they do not quite do.

In these twenty-one pieces of carefully but artificially chosen language, the larger Heaney of the poems, the confessor, the inheritor of the Great Bog, the Romantic in despair before his destiny, disappears. We are left, instead, with twenty-one (to mark a coming of age?) self-conscious entries in a diary of personal memories. And these cut us out by their very artistry. We are left wanting either more autobiography or more art; or perhaps *less* art and more context, more "reality."

An autobiography is not quite art because it purports to be the story of a life. People's lives usually fascinate us, but not as art does. What a man did and thought or wrote, what a person judged funny or sad, what characters molded his/her character, what happened when and why . . . this is the stuff of human and empathetic appetite. We can never get enough of it. But when we are permitted only tiny, exquisite, prechosen fragments of memory, as if in a peepshow, we experience frustration. Curiously, the more beautifully these pieces "read," the more frustrated we feel.

Green air trawled over his arms and legs, the pods and stalks wore a fuzz of light. He caught a rod in each hand and jerked the whole tangle into life. Little tendrils unsprung, new veins lit in the shifting leaves, a caul of shadows stretched and netted round his head again. He sat listening, grateful as the call encroached. ("Cauled")

Primroses grew in a damp single bunch out of the bank, imploding pallors, star plasm, nebula of May. He stared himself into an absence. ("Hedge-school")

Through red seas of July the Orange drummers led a chosen people through their dream . . . The air grew dark, cloud-barred, a butcher's apron. The night hushed like a white-mothed reach of water, miles down-stream from the battle, skeins of blood still lazing in the channel. ("July")

Why, somehow, is the delicacy, the accuracy of these perceptions transformed by their language into sentimentality? Because, I suspect, the writer is writing of childhood experience with an adult eye on his effect. The perception is ingenious but false. The original experiences would not have called forth such eloquence; the language is like paint on an egg.

The importance of *Stations*, then, is that it explodes a contemporary myth we have come too easily to take for granted: the myth of the sensitive self as savior, the myth that the "self" can be salvaged, by art, from failure. What is felicitous in the poems of *North* becomes suspect in the more artificial mode of *Stations*. Perhaps prose-poetry always exhibits this weakness. I think of Oscar Wilde's sentimental fairy tales, of part of *Portraits of the Artist,* when Joyce forgets, momentarily, his genius for the comedy of the tragic. The spectacle of someone feeling sorry for himself or exceptionally tender about his younger self is common; we all cry over our past and love our losses. Heaney is too much of an artist to do that, and yet *Stations* is rosy with held-back tears.

It would be interesting to know whether Heaney wrote "Exposure" before or after *Stations*, for the last Station is called "Incertus," and it seems to fertilize the ground from which "Exposure" sprang. I quote "Incertus" in its entirety.

> I went disguised in it, pronouncing it with a soft church-latin c,
> tagging it under my efforts like a damp fuse. Uncertain. A shy
> soul fretting and all that. Expert obeisance.
>
>   Oh, yes, I crept before I walked. The old pseudonym lies there
> like a mouldering tegument.

If this means that Heaney has left "Incertus" behind him, that he
has found himself enough in the bog poems and "Singing
School" to be able to lose himself, then *Stations is* a station, a
stage in the progress of poet toward mastery of all the material
he calls experience. Still, there is enough evidence, even in
North and *Field Work,* to suggest that "Incertus" is Heaney's worst
enemy. For a man of sensibility and tenderness, it is too easy to
take the soft option of a loving concentration on himself.
Heaney is among the best poets living today, but if he is going to
last, the self-bog, in the end, won't preserve him. It is good to
know that he is translating Dante. That looks like the way out.

III

Other Essays, Reviews, and an Interview

The Trouble with a Word
like *Formalism*

It is no secret that literature since the midcentury has been overshadowed by isms. One hardly needs to list them. At the heels of modernism nipped the New Criticism, which in the 1960s ceded ground, *pace* anthropology, to the sign theory of structuralism. Hardly had we got used to structuralism, when Barthes, Derrida & Co. began to tease us with deconstruction. And now, in the 1990s? In England, you can't so much as glance at a serious literary or intellectual journal without being overcome by a cloud of jargon. The pollution emanates chiefly from a clutter of posts: postmodernism, poststructuralism, postcolonialism, post-Freudianism, post-Marxism, post-Lacanian feminism. One has a sense of living through a postliterary decline; call it interminalism. This essay argues that isms, not to mention post-isms, are the creations of academics, not writers. If we seek to dispel the smoke and rescue poetry from ideology, it would be folly to cover ourselves defensively with academic fug. To me, "the new formalism" feels like fug.

To be fair we have to acknowledge that abstract thinking (as distinct from overtheorizing) has long been vital to literature. If it were simply the job of writers to write and critics to enlighten the public about the nature of writing, few problems would arise. But of course no such simple dichotomy exists. Not many academic critics today dare expose themselves by writing poems, yet their debate about the nature of language has importantly affected contemporary practice. As for the other side, since the time of Aristotle poets have felt compelled to offer the world *apologiae*. In English poetry, Coleridge's criticism claims equality with his verse. Matthew Arnold's perceptions regarding literature and culture are to some extent still relevant. No one presents a better example of a modern critic-poet than T. S. Eliot, whose essays

From *Beyond New Formalism: Essays on Poetic Form and Narrative,* ed. Annie Finch (Brownsville, OR: Story Line Press, 1998). Reprinted with permission.

may be regarded as rational explorations undertaken as relief from the excruciating psychological pressures of making poetry: "the intolerable wrestle with words and meanings."

Formalists may complain that Eliot and the modernists were the source of the trouble, that they are still to blame for the way "difficult" poetry puts people off. Again, anyone who has experienced that "intolerable wrestle" must find such a view facile. Poetry really *is* more difficult to write now than when civilization was younger and artists less self-conscious. The modernist defense still holds: by the turn of the last century it *did* become obvious to the more sensitive that advanced technology—in industry, in communication, in warfare—was about to tear apart the presuppositions of Western society. Changes in traditional forms of living were bound to challenge traditional forms of art. Today, when we look back to the writers who gave radical definition to their feelings after the First World War, it is easy enough to lump them into a category: "the modernists." In actuality, what looks to have been a stylistic revolution represented an extraordinary congruity of response. Everybody was challenged. The most original reacted most vigorously, by "making it new"—and poets naturally "made it new" with language.

Stylistic innovation, then, was a way of showing that new realities demanded new forms. But not only style distinguishes those poets we call "modernists" from "traditionalists" such as Frost and Graves. Both the latter—fine, energetic writers as they were—can be said to have cultivated a dying garden. Frost preserved his growly Yankee voice by holing up north of Boston and writing almost exclusively of (old) rural, not (new) urban experience. Graves disappeared into his own readings of archetypal mythologies. The modernists (Pound, Eliot, Joyce, Stevens), on the other hand, broke with tradition (or a better metaphor perhaps, pruned it back to its roots) in order to renew it.

Three-quarters of a century later it is as important for us to reassess that poetry of innovation as it was for Pound to attack the pastorals of the Georgians. Yet it is incumbent upon us, too, not to oversimplify what modernism meant—not, that is, to treat the modernists (or the Georgians, or the Romantics either) in blocks as "a good thing" or "a bad thing" as if they were items in a literary *1066 and All That*. We would do better instead to examine our own attitudes toward particular poems: to ask ourselves, for example, why *some* of *The Cantos* satisfy us while others do not; or why reading the poems of Wallace Stevens with a fresh eye for their strengths and weaknesses is worth any amount of poring over heaps of criticism. What I am advocating, in short, is an approach to poetry that resembles the creative process itself. Why not read as we would write—aloud for the feeling of speech sounds and the subtleties of rhythm? Let's freely admit to liking or disliking actual poems without labeling them first. Let's approach poetry boldly, at first hand, without recourse to specialist introductions that suggest, in many cases, that a poet's *name* summarizes some inflexible position in a hierarchy of importance.

If readers of poetry (a group that must include everyone who hopes to write it) could free their minds of the stereotyped universals so dear to theorizers, they would be in a better position to understand how the form of a successful poem embodies its meaning. In a good poem, as everybody knows, form is inseparable from sense and tone. No poem worthy of the name can be formless, whether it is written according to metrical rules or in free verse. The sounds, rhythms, pitch, and intensity of the lines ARE the poem. Every poem IS its form. A bad or failed poem is one whose form has either been too much imposed upon it, or neglected through ignorance and lack of an ear—or perhaps because the poet just didn't bring it off. (Shakespeare himself wrote some pretty indifferent verse.)

The trouble with a word like *formalism* is that it seems to impose restrictions on the making of poetry without taking into consideration the conditions a poem sets for itself. As Douglas Dunn commented recently, "There are other ways of making well than those of versification, and, at times, I've suspected that too heavy an emphasis on the technical side of poetry reduces it to the level of car maintenance or flower arranging." Significantly, Dunn goes on, "But what versification offers the writer and reader is a constant re-engagement with the artistry of the past. Conducting that creative investigation in the present could—or so I'd like to believe—help to articulate contemporary life without too much of the dishonour of bad craftsmanship."[1]

Dunn's untrammeled attitude of mind toward "the artistry of the past" keeps the door open to the present. It is perhaps only possible to begin afresh by keeping poetry's roots alive while encouraging it to put forth new branches. By now, though, those roots are so deep and so built over that many are forgotten. The English intellectual tradition that modernism is accused of foisting on us (let's avoid that overused and meaningless term *canon*) extends back to Greek metrics and Latin hexameters on one hand and to Anglo-Saxon kennings on the other. It embraces the medieval poets (those who wrote in Latin, and those who wrote Middle English), then Chaucer, then the Elizabethans and the metaphysicals. No one with an ear for speech rhythms would underestimate, either, the pervasive influence of the King James Bible. I myself would add an unfashionable plea for Milton's noble iambics. So by the time we arrive at the formal metrics of the eighteenth and nineteenth centuries, we are looking back over a long, nourishing heritage of variant patterns—and that before we even approach the Americans and the influence that, after Whitman, American English has wielded everywhere in the world.

Any valid ideology behind formalism, one must suppose, would encompass all such patterns as models. Yet the term is pretty well doomed to misinterpretation in the present world, in which historical imagination and sensibility play so small a part. Uninformed people of a politically correct persuasion are bound to associate a term like *formalism* with political conservatism—as, in another context, Douglas Dunn sharply points out.[2]

More importantly, many well-meaning contemporaries use the term formalism as if it meant merely writing in rhyme and meter—merely learning to scan, or count syllables and stresses so as to qualify as a producer of sonnets, couplets, narrative epics, and so on. Alas, most beginners who try out "form" in poetry achieve only exercises in verse—probably not very good verse at that. They would almost certainly write better poetry if they followed their instincts in free verse, if free verse is what they were brought up hearing. It's not so much that poetic technique or craft cannot be taught (it can and should be) as that the process of absorbing and assimilating the feel of poetry is so psychologically complex. It takes a long time—half a lifetime maybe—to *overhear* those hardly definable facets of a language that give it a distinctive music. Writing poetry is inseparable from a poet's unconscious at homeness with the sounds, inflections, pitches, and textures of a language. The pulse of its rhythms, the different weights and lengths of its vowels—these have to accumulate in a poet's consciousness without his knowing how. Hence, the mysterious instinctual element that tradition associates with the muse. Inspiration truly does make poetry possible. And that is why, as many poets have testified, "creative writing" cannot be taught, and why a real poem almost always feels like a donnée when it arrives.

Yet despite the temptations of metaphor, there is really nothing organic about poetry. Keats never said that poetry was a tree; he said that unless poetry *comes to the poet as easily as leaves to the tree* it had better not come at all. The emphasis is all on the poet's unconscious mind which, *like* a tree, roots itself in common verbal experience and yet creates, in verse, memorable patterns of language. Keats listened to the rhythms of "past artistry" in Shakespeare and Spenser; the leaves he put forth derived from his passional instinct for knowing what music to overhear and what words to write down. Such a practice requires a different order of self-discipline from mechanically counting syllables or stresses in a line, or learning to tell the difference between iambic and anapestic feet.

Robert Wells, a contemporary English poet who is acutely conscious of form, suggests that, for him, writing poetry is the result of a personal need to get something clear. What lures him on, he says, "is the promise of form which allows that to happen." Clarification means finding a form of language that will tell him what he feels. Earlier in the same essay, he writes:

> It may be possible to look at the result [of a poem] and detect a set of principles at work, but in the actual writing I'm simply out to please myself. Within the form I've chosen I work entirely by ear, and choosing the form too is largely a matter for the ear, of hearing the potential for shape within a body of material which may itself be only vaguely apprehended, so that I have the form of a poem sometimes before I discover the content.

And he goes on,

> The terminology of meter provides a useful way of describing poems once they are written, but I seldom feel the need for it

when writing. I will count syllables and listen for pauses, but I've never asked myself in so many words whether an iamb or trochee is required in such-and-such a place, or where the caesura should occur in a particular line. The work of getting the poem right is done by the ear, or rather by the ear and voice together, as one hears oneself when one is speaking. Of course, the ear's instinct isn't an innocent one. Reading, observations and practice all play their part in it.[3]

Where, then, is your need for formalism? The case for form is won with every good poem that's written—and then sensitively read by readers who can judge for themselves whether it is worth rereading. What should be taught are techniques of reading such as actors learn when they study Shakespeare, or children used to be taught when they were encouraged to recite poems in primary school. If, as may happen, the culture of the past is wholly lost and our children grow up knowing nothing of literature but the popular entertainments they see on television, there will be no point at all in teaching them to write in archaic meters. The rules of English metrics were, in any case, derived from the long- and short-vowel patterns of Greek and Latin verse; they have never perfectly adapted to the stress patterns of English.

As long as poetry remains part of our culture (and there's an awful lot of it about these days) *some* poets will write by ear. In the distant past, poetry was primarily heard.[4] Today a lot is published (pretty much of it mediocre) that relies purely on imagery or, in periodicals like the *Times Literary Supplement,* on fairly obscure insider references and allusions. Meanwhile, new poetries—from the Caribbean, for example, and from Africa and Australia—are introducing new rhythms into English and enhancing its vitality. The English poetry of the future is bound to take on and mix influxes from even more cultures. What a mistake it would be—how impossible it already *is*—to attempt to channel the flood within the narrow banks of traditional form, in the most limited, archaic sense of that formula. The best poetry of the past will last as long as readers read it; and it will last the longer if it is not forced to retreat or (to change the metaphor) inbreed but instead is encouraged to take its chances in a changing world and survive by adapting.

NOTES

1. "Public and private realms—a comment on his new collection from Douglas Dunn," in *The Poetry Book Society Bulletin* 159 (winter 1993): 12.

2. Douglas Dunn, "Writing Things Down," in *The Poet's Voice and Craft,* ed. C. B. McCully (Manchester: Carcanet, 1994), 100.

3. Robert Wells, "Distinctive Anonymity," in McCully, *Poet's Voice and Craft,* 168.

4. For a thorough exposition of this view, see Francis Berry, *Poetry and the Physical Voice* (London: Oxford University Press, 1962), esp. chap. 1, "Problems of Hearing and Saying."

Poetry and Place

Our notions of place, like those of time, are evidently indivisible from language, for our ideas of duration and geographical boundary must themselves be functions of our minds. Devoid of human beings and human history, this life-bearing planet would exist, though without us it could not be the earth we know. Inferring the absence of a creative Deity, twentieth-century intellectuals have been tempted to claim a great deal for themselves. We've heard it suggested, with some reason, that language *invents* the world (from the Latin *invenire,* to find); and so, by extension, that words, in a sense, create what they name. From such challenging premises, the poet Wallace Stevens seems to have concluded that though we partake of and depend upon nature we can only make it meaningful through our imaginations. The imagination's artifacts (such as words and works of art) organize what we see and provide us with what we know. To me, Stevens's "Anecdote of the Jar" still represents an iconoclastic shattering of long-held assumptions.

In three economical stanzas, Stevens sets forth as plainly as possible the intriguing puzzle, or miracle, of how art organizes nature. And not only art. Could not that jar on a hill in Tennessee be a twelfth-century castle in Wales, a nineteenth-century water tower in Cambridgeshire, an observation deck on the top of a California mountain? For Stevens it was above all an aesthetic jar. The eighth line, "And tall and of a port in air," suggests, perhaps, im*port*ance—or better, de*port*ment, bearing. The artificial, aesthetic bearing of the jar exalts human craft over geographical place. It provides incontrovertible evidence of humankind's creative ascendancy.

"Port," too, implies the achievement of a refuge from nature: a harbor, a safe airport. The line focuses on ambiguity in a way

---

From a lecture given at an International Symposium on Poetry and Place organized by the University of Tübingen, 1990. First published in *Regionalität, Nationalität und Internationalität in der zeitgenössischen Lyrik— Erträge des Siebten Blaubeurer Symposions,* ed. Lothar Fietz, Paul Hoffman, and Hans Werner Ludwig (Tübingen: Attempto Verlag, 1992).

that is characteristic of Stevens at his best, directing the reader straight to the bald statement of "It took dominion everywhere." Anyone who enjoys climbing or walking in the mountains will know how it feels suddenly to encounter signs of human dominion—a signpost, for example, or a stile over a wall. A mountain hostel is welcome for the shelter it provides, consoling because it confirms the interdependence of the human species, but at the same time disconcertingly unnatural. And if the human artifacts there encountered include piles of rusting tins and discarded plastic, one's sense of human dominion is likely to be outraged.

Such experiences are familiar. As we humans increasingly multiply and take "dominion everywhere," we are less and less able to cherish the delicate interdependency that still exists— for we are natural creatures despite our computer-like brains— between the places we make and the natural environment that brought us about in the first place. Something like Heisenberg's principle in particle physics comes into operation with every attempt we make to understand the wilderness. It is practically impossible for human beings to observe a state of nature without in some measure—a track through the underbrush, a circle of rocks around a fire—changing it.

This is not to advocate a romantic view. As even the keenest environmentalists have to admit, nature cultivated is pleasanter to live in than nature raw. As people, as citizens, we have to learn to preserve the balance of nature on this planet, or we'll perish. Yet for writers, the notion of a poetry of place is often more abstract. When I find poetry in places—as I often do—I'm always aware, somewhere at the back of my mind, of the teasing paradox suggested by Stevens. If what we experience as a place is no more than what we imaginatively see or invent, how can we *really* know anywhere? In a sense, the better we seem to know a place, the less aware we are of that intriguing unknown—the world that does exist, and could always have existed, without us.

For the Mexican poet Octavio Paz, the unknown perpetually hovers at the margins of the knowable. A poem of his called "January First"—translated by Paz himself, with Elizabeth Bishop— moves from one side of Stevens's equation to the other. On New Year's Eve a woman says to her husband in true Stevensian fashion, "Tomorrow, we shall have to invent, / once more, / the reality of this world." Next morning, however, the poet wakes to discover that reality has been invented already.

> Time, with no help from us,
> had placed
> in exactly the same order as yesterday
> houses in the empty street,
> snow on the houses,
> silence on the snow.

Remembering how his wife had slept on, unconscious under his gaze, he turns her proposition inside out: "The day had invented you," he says, "but you hadn't yet accepted being invented by the day. . . . You were in another day." Unconsciousness the poem implies, is a condition of passivity, a state of mind in which the brain may act reflectively (as in dreaming) while active memory, or that facet of the mind that invents what it empirically perceives, is suppressed. To the conscious observer, the sleeper appears to be an object created, not by perception but by time. The other operative word in the poem is *appearances*.

> You were beside me
> and I saw you, like the snow,
> asleep among appearances.
> Time, with no help from us,
> invents houses, streets, trees
> and sleeping women.

Now, there's a great deal of difference—isn't there?— between saying with Stevens that the imagination "creates" the houses, streets, and people one lives among, and saying with Paz that time "with no help from us" invents appearances—even when the mind isn't looking. Paz, in other words, makes allowances for a metaphysical dimension, an enticing realm of the unknown, that Stevens, inspired apologist for imagination that he is, does not. Paz's poem continues:

> When you open your eyes
> we'll walk, once more,
> among the hours and their inventions.
> We'll walk among appearances

and bear witness to time and its conjugations.
Perhaps we'll open the day's doors.
And then we shall enter the unknown.

Now, we might agree that whether the world is created by
time or by imagination is not a question either poet would want
to fight over in the academic journals. It is difficult to deny these
days that the actual world we inhabit has been and is being
naturally selected by eon-long processes of evolution. Poetry,
though, has the advantage over science in being able to enter-
tain and accept a number of contradictory hypotheses. In any
case, poetry is a mode of expression, not epistemological proof.
It is perhaps worth suggesting that any philosophical argument
between these two would have to focus on the meaning of "the
unknown." For Stevens, any supernatural existence must by defi-
nition be unknowable, and therefore of little interest to the
active, creative mind. For Paz, the unknown relates, probably, to
a presumed mystical state beyond human comprehension, in
the presence of which the mind would have to be passive.

My point here is that for the purposes of poetry either phi-
losophy will do. The lines I want to emphasize in Paz's poem are
these: "We'll walk among appearances / and *bear witness* to time
and its conjugations." The notion that poets *bear witness* to
changes (time's conjugations) in the world they experience sug-
gests that a two-way line between subject and object must be
established. A two-way circuit, as in the creation of electricity,
comes into being as soon as the poet acknowledges that he or
she and the world are simultaneously inventing each other.

The negative pole in this circuit (Keats's "negative capabil-
ity") relates to a poet's capacity to receive, a willingness continu-
ally to be impressed, or "invented." To be open to impressions,
as every poet of real sensibility knows, protects the explorative
mind from stagnation, from choking itself on obsessive interior
concerns. As one who bears witness, the poet must, as Keats
knew, keep alive the child within the adult—keep some impres-
sionable core green and curious. This quality of receptiveness,
of being continually aware, tends to fade as one grows older.
The world—in the sense of society—has little time for people it
cannot identify as types or confine to categories. It wants to
invent us in our youth and then appoint us as adults to get on

with its business. But the modern poet's business is painfully to resist climbing into preestablished pigeonholes. At risk of offending an oversocialized world, poets, to preserve unsocialized realities, have to insist that something—time or experience—invents them over and over again. The world, as it were, is never let off the hook. The poet is continually putting it on the spot, challenging its terms, reinventing, magnifying, even distorting it by means of the positive element in the creative exchange.

This positive element in the circuit is nothing less than what we call creative imagination or creative energy, and when it unexpectedly produces a new idea or way of expressing a truth, the world stands back amazed and shouts "Genius!" From the poet's point of view (and I should say, also, that of any original thinker) a successful act of creation resembles nothing so much as a breakthrough—sometimes with agonizing psychological effects—from something *outside* one's normal range of understanding into some inner and active source of language. To produce a "real" poem and not simply an imitative exercise, an element of the unknown has to enter into the poet's labor of sifting through the available syntax, overhearing linear rhythms, and generally experimenting with words and sounds. To witness a poem in the act of creating itself, to watch it excavate and identify some buried matter of the unconscious, or find original language for mute experience, can be exhilarating beyond belief. No one who has experienced the excitement of "really writing," as Sylvia Plath called it, can ever bear to contemplate giving it up.

You may want to complain that this paper, purporting to be about poetry and place, has thus far laid too much emphasis on what I have termed the creative circuit. Nothing, however, is more important to the making of poetry than that simultaneous input and output of mental energy which, like electricity, will only turn you on when both negative and positive poles are connected and functioning. It is my guess that once you are familiar with what it means to be caught up in such a circuit, once you have experienced its addictive satisfaction, nothing the world can offer in the way of alternatives is likely to deter you—if you are a poet—from seeking a way of life that provides a more or less reliable creative generator. Perhaps, indeed, we should change the electrical metaphor and instead compare the attractions of an ongoing creative current with sexual pleasure.

Poets radically differ, of course, as to which conditions best set off the necessary, irresistible two-way exchange of energy. Negative input need not arrive via the phenomena of worldly appearances. A philosophy, a religion, a mystical revelation, a personal story, an obsession with the past or with human behavior—any stimulating factor passionately absorbed will activate the circuit. Wallace Stevens, for example, made a comparatively easy compromise with the external world, for it concerned him as a poet chiefly as it embodied certain passionately held ideas. As these ideas related to his aesthetic sensibility, not really to particular places, he traveled no further than Florida and made a good living as an executive of a large insurance company in Hartford. The quiet man, Wallace Stevens, evidently contrived to live in comfortably settled surroundings well suited to the requirements of the energetic poet.

Similarly, Marianne Moore collected most of her images— those wonderful animals and artifacts she painstakingly embroidered into the moral fancywork of her art—from junk shops, circuses, sportsgrounds, local newspapers, and the New York Public Library. Arthur Waley, whose translations from the Chinese poets are still classics of their kind, refused to visit China on the excellent grounds that the China that inspired him no longer existed and perhaps never had, save in many fanciful journeys of the mind. On the other hand, there have always been poets who have found creation impossible without continuous erotic or masochistic excitement. For Baudelaire, the sleazier quarters of Paris providentially provided the right "place" for the cultivation of *Les Fleurs du Mal*. It shows no disrespect to poets or poetry to suggest that, however disadvantaged by poverty and mental disorder, they have for centuries converted personal misfortune into creative necessity. So much so, indeed, that the accepted image of the poet, even today, is associated in the public mind with demonic behavior and early, fated death or self-destruction.

Fortunately, not every muse is tragic, and poets have in many cases found ways of keeping the wires live without overcharging the emotional exchange and blowing fuses. Not that despair is ever far away, for the energy available for poetry capriciously depends on unconscious factors, many of which constitute truly negative—however receptive—elements in the creative circuit. Such negative sources of power suggest ironically that the suppression of poetic freedom in the U.S.S.R. and countries behind the Iron Curtain during the middle years of this century in some cases produced "better" creative conditions for artists—even if the price was martyrdom—than has the philistine capitalism of the West.

For us, a powerful "free" press, advertising, and the overwhelming influence of television have tended to promote an atmosphere of marketable triviality that is difficult for an artist to overcome. For no matter how bravely poets battle for independence, no matter what eccentricities they hide behind or freedom they demand for their souls, they cannot but feel answerable to *some* social group for which they write. By definition, a poet has to belong, if not to a particular nation or geographical place, at least to a historical context. There is no poetry without a language, and if the culture inherited at birth does not answer to creative needs, then the poet has to set out in quest of one that does.

In most cases, there is something in a poet's past—his roots in a village, a family, a religion, a long acquaintance with a particular city—that will remain a source of energy even if he exiles himself—or because he exiles himself. James Joyce is a supreme example. Writing *Ulysses* in Paris and retreating at the end of his life to Zürich, he was never other than Irish in his imagination. His compatriot, Samuel Beckett, presents, perhaps, a more complex case. Claustrophobic, parochial Ireland was as inimical to Beckett's gift as it was to Joyce's. Yet Beckett's field of reference—psychological and existential—makes no concessions to Dublin or to Irishness—or so it appears. (Although whether Beckett or Joyce is the more "universal" artist is a moot point; and both are Irish in the sense that no other nation, probably, could account for them.)

The fact is, we are not given much choice as to where or how to live if keeping the creative circuit alive predetermines our behavior. A writer (say, Sylvia Plath) may set out by rejecting her home environment and going off to a place that nourishes her imagination. But ten to one what she'll write about when she gets there is the very situation that drove her away. For, as a poet, it is one thing to seek out a place you can write *in,* quite another to remain faithful in your poetry to those inexorable psychological factors that make writing a necessity. There are poets of whom Pascal would have approved, who scarcely stirred from their houses. Others, not less provided with imaginative talent, have had to put distance between themselves and their origins. In Elizabeth Bishop's case, restlessness occasionally produced something like an apology. At the end of her poem "Questions of Travel" she asks:

> *"Is it lack of imagination that makes us come*
> *to imagined places, not just stay at home?*
> *Or could Pascal have been not entirely right*
> *about just sitting quietly in one's room?*
>
> *Continent, city, country, society:*
> *the choice is never wide and never free.*
> *And here, or there . . . No, should we have stayed at home,*
> *wherever that may be?"*

"The choice is never wide and never free." And then, too, Elizabeth Bishop would have been the first to acknowledge that her choice of where to go and what to look for never wholly depended on her art. Like other people, poets travel out of curiosity or a liking for adventure. They fall in love with the people of (or a person in) another country. They are offered jobs they can't refuse. They are driven from home by intolerable personal or political conditions, or they are attracted to foreign places by sheer illusion. Questions of travel rarely get simple answers. But if you ask a poet *why* the choice of where to live cannot be wide or free, the answer is likely to touch on the negative/positive creative exchange I have tried to identify. Given sufficient financial latitude and freedom from external pressures, a poet will consciously or unconsciously choose to live in an environment that best activates that personal creative generator.

A Chev'ril Glove

> *Clown.* . . . To see this age! A sentence is but a chev'ril glove to a
> good wit: how quickly the wrong side may be turned
> outward.
> *Viola.* Nay, that's certain; they that dally nicely with words may
> quickly make them wanton.
> *Clown.* I would therefore my sister had no name, sir.
> *Viola.* Why, man?
> *Clown.* Why, sir, her name's a word, and to dally with that word
> might make my sister wanton. But indeed, words are very
> rascals since bonds disgraced them.
> *Viola.* Thy reason, man?
> *Clown.* Truth, sir, I can yield you none without words, and words
> are grown so false I am loath to prove reason with them.
> —Shakespeare, *Twelfth Night*

I have been asked to identify some of the structural questions with which I engage when I write poems. How conscious am I of metrical considerations? Are my poems constructed according to bonds of meter and rhythm, or do I pay more attention to sound-affinities and textures? Do I attempt in verse to reproduce the rhythmical structure of colloquial speech? Do I write by phrase or clause, with nouns and adjectives or chiefly with verbs? On what principle do I choose words, seek rhymes, re-write, revise, and in other ways consciously preside over the process of making poetry?

Now, frankly, I do not believe anyone sitting down with a like set of questions could write a poem. At best one might produce a pastiche or an experiment, a poetic exercise. And yet structural considerations can never, ever be ignored! Theorists sometimes take delight in mystifying the complicated game of language that poets take delight in playing. And poets are usually ready enough to make exaggerated claims for themselves. The truth is that critics and poets alike have to acknowledge poetry's

---

From *The Poet's Voice and Craft,* ed. C. B. McCully (Manchester: Carcanet Press, 1994). Reprinted with permission.

long, vigorous, independent existence. Every poem worthy of the name is a personal artifact made of public language, and it is only the foolish who refuse to acknowledge that questions of prosody arise immediately the first cadences of a poem have shouldered themselves into existence.

Let me briefly translate that declaration into personal experience. Like many poets, I began to write verse when I was introduced to Shakespeare and the English Romantics as a child. I have no doubt that it was rhythm, the stressed, unstressed undulations of the iambic line, that first bewitched me. In those pretelevision days, my parents often spent companionable evenings reading aloud to us children and to each other. Mother read history and fiction; my father read poetry, and we all took parts in the more accessible of Shakespeare's comedies. I especially remember my father, an amateur musician, reading with fervor Scott's *Marmion* and *The Lady of the Lake*, Coleridge's *Ancient Mariner*, Arnold's "The Forsaken Merman" and "Sorhab and Rustum," Browning's "My Last Duchess," Lord Macaulay's "Horatius at the Bridge." Then, at ten or eleven, I was taught by an eccentric English teacher who insisted that her pupils learn poems by heart. One by one, we had to stand up and recite to the class. I discovered that learning poems came easily to me. Before long I was cultivating a reputation as top reciter of the sixth grade. Poetry was something I could do, something that in part made up for my woeful inability to understand what was going on in arithmetic.

I began writing ballads and plays when I was twelve or so, but in my teens I became a thoroughgoing Romantic, imagining fondly that I was an incarnation of the poet Keats, whose odes and sonnets I imitated, along with those of Edna St. Vincent Millay. My first poems, I believe, were romantically inspired on two counts. I responded instinctively to the rhythms, language, and heroic subjects of romantic English verse; and I created an image of myself as artist that suspended me in my own myth as I drifted through school, dreaming of future laurels. Fortunately, three excellent English teachers at the University High School in Ann Arbor taught me to write prose and (up to a point) to spell. They gave me Ds for carelessness and As for imagination, and they minded not at all if I imitated Shakespeare, writing and directing my own plays. (Nothing was ever said, either explicitly or by implication, about any handicap I might have incurred through the misfortune of having been born female.)

In 1950 I graduated from high school and entered the university to study not English but music, later French and history. In that same year an anthology was published that challenged many of my ideas about poetry. I still possess a tattered paperback copy of *New Poets of England and America,* edited by Donald Hall and Robert Pack. In it, Auden-like precepts of order, intelligibility, good manners, and responsibility for the world outside oneself set the tone for what looked like a twentieth-century return to classicism.

At Michigan, impressed by John Ciardi, the first "real" poet I'd met, I began to write lyrical poems in the manner of Frost and Richard Wilbur (then very popular) and also of a famous young woman called Adrienne Cecile Rich. The latter, only a little older than myself, won the Yale Series of Younger Poets prize in 1951, and like Sylvia Plath (of whom I then knew nothing) I was both envious and in awe of her. In several early poems I tried to emulate her suave, disciplined, informal, very accessible style. (Adrienne Rich today may view those early successes with feminist contempt.)

During the same years of the early 1950s, I was working closely with composers, painters, dancers, and actors at Michigan in a student organization called the Inter-Arts Union. Most of my literary productions of that time were dramatic and eclectic: a masque for dancing in the manner of Ben Jonson, or possibly Yeats; an Auden-like libretto for a one-act opera, *Adam and Eve and the Devil;* lyrics and conversational monologues in the style of Robert Frost. As a junior I learned enough Italian to take a course in Dante. Several of my avant-garde contemporaries worshiped Ezra Pound—whom I privately thought a charlatan. (I was wrong!) Others were wild about Eliot, whose weary, sophisticated tone I chose to imitate in preference to the inflamed rhetoric of Dylan Thomas. But particular "influences" probably mattered less than the ardent excitement a group of us experienced as "artists." We felt ourselves, my friends and I, to be in the forefront of the modernist movement. The blood jet was not so much poetry as a fountain of unbounded creative energy. I half believed, in those days, that art could save—if not the world—at least me in the world, or me from the world.

Soon after I left the university, I married and moved to England. My enthusiasm for modernism waned as I became painfully acquainted with the realities of postwar English life and culture, and for seven or eight years I was too confused to write anything. A poem called "The Women" slipped idly from me in Yorkshire in 1956. I sent it to *Poetry Chicago,* where it was published, but it was not until 1961, when I met Donald Hall after returning to Michigan, that I became aware of a new and nourishing climate in American verse. The poets—apart from Hall himself—to whom I listened when I began to write again were Wallace Stevens, Robert Lowell, Louis Simpson, Marianne Moore, and especially Elizabeth Bishop. Elizabeth Bishop's poems pleased me so much I undertook, as a graduate student, to write a short book on her work. My own first collection of poems, *Living in America,* owes a great deal to discoveries I made about diction, tone, pitch, and content in poetry in the course of studying first Hall and then Bishop.

Now Elizabeth Bishop, although famous for her painterly eye, confessed to me once that, unlike Marianne Moore, she felt herself to be an old-fashioned, "umpty-umpty" poet. A mentor of hers—who also became mine—was the seventeenth-century English metaphysical, George Herbert. Bishop was familiar with and very fond of Baptist hymns; she was a fan of ballad meters and folk tunes—see her "Songs for a Colored Singer" and "The Burglar of Babylon." Besides, she was contagiously in love with the natural world and with adventure and travel. Without being at all academic, she was an admirer of Darwin, an amateur expert on contemporary art, a devout reader of cookbooks, a lover of landscapes and languages, with a mind always ready to be entertained by the sheer quiddity and oddity of the world. In short, she was for me, though no dramatist, a minor Shakespearean writer.

Think what a magpie Shakespeare was, picking up scraps and tatters of usable language from street and tavern, court and countryside, lawbooks and chronicle. His little Latin and less Greek were inessential items discarded from a huge working stock of English with which he furnished and embellished a mental studio of inconceivable proportions. I like to think of Shakespeare, of poets in general, inhabiting a world like a warehouse, a factory floor full of molten language and malleable forms, who are always a little impatient with the ways of scholars and libraries, who get bored in museums of sacred phrases and run like crazy at the appearance of high-sounding academic theories.

Elizabeth Bishop, to me, was that kind of working poet, and from her, as from Donald Hall, I learned—not how to write poetry, but how to handle the material laid out on the workshop floor. My first "real" book of poems, *Reversals,* fell all but dead from Wesleyan University Press in 1969. Yet I felt that in writing it, I had set myself a certain standard of economy and craft. Here's a love poem from that early collection. My love poems, I'm afraid, usually reveal feelings of ambiguity. The trick here was to catch a shift of vision in sound as well as word.

Aubade

Intervention of chairs at midnight.
The wall's approach, the quirkish ambivalence
of photographs, today in daylight,
mere pieces of balance. My brown dress,
tossed, messed, upheld by the floor.
Rags of ordinary, washed light
draped as to dry on the brown furniture.
And the big bed reposed, utterly white
that ached our darkness, rocked our weight.

You can see that it was important to rhyme, but not always closely: midnight/daylight/ white/weight; ambivalence/brown dress; floor/furniture. There is no line-ending that doesn't chime with some other, although the rhyme scheme is irregular. And having been strict with the rhymes, I let the cadences fall where they would, only restricting the lines to four or five stresses each. The meter is loosely iambic/trochaic, but so is the English language generally. The inner rhymes on an *s* sound— pieces, dress, tossed, messed—were arrived at, as it were, accidentally, in the course of writing. I couldn't, of course, have predicted any of the formal features of the poem before it began to sing of itself.

My first English collection (*Travelling behind Glass,* 1974) included a number of longish, free-verse meditations that rhythmically imitated Auden or Eliot, though now they sound to me more like MacNeice. In sections of a poem called "England" for instance, the pulse beats are discursively iambic, with lots of enjambment.

Americans like England to live in her cameo,
A dignified profile attached to a past
Understood to belong to her, like the body of a bust.
The image to the native is battered but complete,
The cracked clay flaking, reluctantly sloughed away,
Inadequately renewed on her beautiful bones.

The stinginess of England. The proliferating ugliness.
The pale boys, harmful, dissatisfied, groping for comfort
In the sodium darkness of December evenings.
Wet roofs creeping for miles along wet bricks.

(I like, even today, to startle the reader with a short, sharp line, set off from a ruminating description or argument.)

Lovers urgently propping each other on the endless
Identical pavements in the vacant light
Where the cars live, their pupilless eyes
Turning upward without envy or disapproval.

Unfortunately, my original conclusion of "England" subsided into banal philosophy. One of the better bits, however, records a mood of personal resignation (as I now see but didn't, consciously, then) by breaking off the literary syntax and addressing someone (a friend, a lover) directly.

September. Already autumnal.
Lost days drift in shapes under the plane trees.
Leaves tangle in the gutters.
In Greenwich, in Kew, in Hampstead
The paths are dry, the ponds dazed with reflections.
Come with me. Look. The city
Nourished by its poisons, is beautiful in them.
A pearly contamination strokes the river
As the cranes ride or dissolve in it,
And the sun dissolves in the hub of its own explosion.

The whole poem, imperfect as it seems to me now, depends for its effect on lyrical cadences I would be hard put to notate. I still write poems by overhearing the rhythms of what I used to call "inevitable cadences." I suspect I simply remember the rhythms of poems learned in childhood, and any violation of those rhythms sounds wrong.

After 1966 or so, when I wrote "England," I conscientiously tried to break away from an inherited lyrical tradition (abandoning, incidentally, the convention of beginning each line of a poem with an uppercase letter), swinging toward Carlos Williams's colloquial three-line stanza in some of the dramatic monologues of *Correspondences* (1974); working toward a freer, more cursive discipline of line in *Enough of Green* (1977). Questions of style are not, of course, matters of choice. The rhythm of what has to be said determines, in the end, how it *will* be said. The lusher poems of *Minute by Glass Minute,* for instance, were dictated both by a state of mind and the landscape of the Wye valley, on the border between England and Wales. In *The Fiction-Makers* I gave rein to a taste for irony and an increasingly strong belief that a clear distinction must be made between art and life.

Many changes of attitude over the years—debates with myself about the place and importance of poetry, of language itself (the central debate, to be sure, of the age we live in)—have not, I think, affected the way I begin working on a poem once a line or a tune has taken root. A given rhythm is usually primary, though an idea may hang around for months before it announces the rhythm in which it must be treated.

I am myself, of course, harder to please these days. Instead of being overwhelmed by tidal waves of creation, as when younger, I often have to dig hard for nourishment. In the course of digging one becomes especially conscious of words, and, like Feste in *Twelfth Night,* alert to the two-way relationship they establish with their presumed masters. If there is a difference between my assumptions now and those of twenty years ago, it arises from an awareness that the very act of recording experience inevitably distorts it. Fiction and even the factual records we call history should not be confused with the vast complex of feelings we apprehend every moment of our lives through our minds and senses. Any part of the three- or four-dimensional continuum we call experience that we choose to commit to two-dimensional paper (or for that matter, a two-dimensional screen) is fiction making, however convincingly mimetic. The purpose of organized language is to simplify, clarify, define, celebrate, make beautiful or ugly, greater or smaller, certain recognizable physical or psychological events. There is no writing that is more complex than the language it employs, and that language can never be as complicated as the psychological events it stands for. In other words, words can never absolutely tell the truth. I played with this notion in a little poem I take as a serious joke.

> The idea of event is horizontal,
> the idea of personality, vertical.
> Let fiction take root
> in the idea of the cross between them.
>
> The mind of the world
> is a vast field of crosses.
> We pick our way through the cemetery
> calling out names and stories.
>
> In the event
> the story is foretold,
> foremade in the code of its happening.
>
> In the event
> the event is sacrificed
> to a fiction of its having happened.

I am unable to describe the feeling of relief that little poem brought to me. It was like springing the lock on a frame of type and watching the symbols spill out freely on the table; like being taken backstage in the theater of human ideas and shown how many ancient props of language and tradition are still flexibly there for us to use and modify and play with. Never mind the anxiety of influence or the awesome presence of sacred texts, dead geniuses, learned theorists, and the rest. They all have their place in the perpetual play of human imagination. The figure of the poet, in such a perspective, presents itself in its old, Shakespearean guise—Lear's fool, or Feste the jester, her ladyship's "corrupter of words"—who quips and sings his way through living fictions of hierarchy and power, delusion and treachery, vanity and virtue, with the sanctioned liberty of an acknowledged witness. Superficial changes in culture and language over five hundred years or so (less than a second of geological time) have scarcely altered the mythmaking, story-making, fiction-making habits we humans so much need and enjoy.

"All the world's a stage, / And all the men and women merely players," declares the poet Jaques in *As You Like It,* wittily undermining those two recurring fictions of civilization, courtly pomp and pastoral innocence. Yeats sounded the same note toward the end of his life, viewing the human and political crises of his time with eyes "that are always gay."

> All perform their tragic play,
> There struts Hamlet, there is Lear,
> That's Ophelia, that Cordelia;
> Yet they, should the last scene be there,
> The great stage curtain about to drop,
> If worthy their prominent part in the play,
> Do not break up their lines to weep.
> They know that Hamlet and Lear are gay.

It is unfortunate that *gay* has taken on another, specifically sexual connotation in our time; but perhaps here is just another example of how a word can shift in the harness of meaning and turn itself inside out, altering its effect even within the straitjacket of a famous poem. Words, in short, are the poet's servants and the poet's masters, most useful when they are most alive, fallible, and human, but of very little importance when somebody's theory chloroforms them on the page or turns them into textual beasts of burden.

> Irish poets, learn your trade,
> Sing whatever is well made,
> Scorn the sort now growing up
> All out of shape from toe to top.

Enough. Since this paper purports to answer questions relating to my own craft, let me conclude by reading you several passages from a poem I wrote after I had attended a poetry festival in Toronto. I called the poem "Ward's Island," and it describes traveling by ferry, on a freezing winter's day, from the city to an offshore island on Lake Ontario. Ward's Island was, I'm told, the site of the first trapper's settlement in the area, but it is now—or was when I visited it—a public park bordered by a group of shabby little houses the municipal council, I believe, is trying to get rid of. It was minus eighteen degrees centigrade when I landed on the island, and I walked for about an hour, first inland, and then along the freezing outer shore, where the lapping waves had coated the rounded rocks with ice. I thought at the time, "This is the end of the world, this is what it will be like."

I scratched some lines in my notebook on my return trip: "waves like fishscales / Brutality of the skyscrapers, blunt-topped metal coffins, all of them banks. The five colours of the city's opulence: silver, jet, gold, burgundy, jade. Ward's little island survives, with its down-at-heels shanties of clapboard and synthetic brick, broken toys, rusty iron chairs, lonely cat etc.—what sort of community?"

It must have been March when I sat down, finally, to make something of these fragments. One line especially pleased me: "silver, jet, gold, porphyry, jade" (I substituted *porphyry* for *burgundy* so as to keep the stone/metal imagery consistent). Using it as a rhythmic base, I soon had a stanza.

> A sunny Sunday, cobalt, with feathery clouds.
> Wind at minus eighteen degrees centigrade
> knifing the lake. I felt on my face
> the grinding of its blade. But water tossed light
> like fish scales in our wake, so I stayed on deck
> in my boots and visible breath
> watching the city recede, its rich brocade
> silver, jet, gold, porphyry, jade.

The poem was clearly going to be longish and discursive, with sharp points of rhyme here and there, internal rhymes (centigrade/blade/recede/brocade) and also end-rhymes. The casual tone would eventually determine, within a loose syntax, what its exact diction should be. I worked for several days to set pace and tone within a framework of firm or near rhymes.

> I heard my footsteps one by one talk *back*
> along a windswept municipal *boardwalk:*
> evergreens, benches, tourist views of the *lake.*

(Here I struggled, unconsciously, to shift back and forth from sure masculine line-endings to more tentative feminine ones.)

> On the other side, the open side, colder.
> I saw how ice had hugged and hugged each boulder;
> the beach was studded with layered, glittering skulls.
> I kept on walking, with whatever it was I felt—
> something between jubilation and fear.
> There appeared to be no traffic at all
> on that sea no one could see over;
> only to the airport frail, silver insects
> sailed from the beautiful air.

After the absolute rhyme of colder and boulder, sound affinities between skulls/felt/all, and of fear/appeared/frail/air, seemed sufficient to sustain the music during this climactic section of the poem. You'll notice a distortion of normal syntax: "only to the airport frail, silver insects / sailed from the beautiful air." Think of the banality of writing instead, "the only activity I could see were far-away silver airplanes, like insects, flying in and silently landing."

I'm still pleased with the last lines of "Ward's Island," in which I found I could pursue an ambiguity already established in an earlier stanza with the word "banks"—that is, banks of the lake and banks full of money. Here are the final lines of the poem:

> Still, I caught the next ferry back.
> A gaunt youth in a baseball cap and two burly men
> settled themselves and their boredom
> in the too hot cabin,
> there to spread newsprint wings and disappear.
> I paced the warmth, rubbing life into my hands.
> The city advanced to meet us, cruel and dear.

Here, not only was I able to refer obliquely to the ethereal planes—those silver insects sailing from the air—by making these bored men "spread newsprint wings," but I could use a colloquial expression, "rub life into my [freezing] hands" to indicate the preciousness of life on any terms. And the final line is ambiguous on two counts: "The city advanced to meet us, cruel and dear." "Advanced" describes the apparent movement of the city toward the ferry as it nears the harbor; at the same time, the word suggests that the city is "advanced," that is, in an advanced state of civilization. The words "cruel and dear," of course, play with the advantages and disadvantages of advanced living; *dear* means expensive as well as precious. Which is precisely the kind of ambiguity I desired to express during the actual experience of traveling to the island.

I have to say that, for me, "Ward's Island" succeeds as a poem. It derives from actual experience and expresses something of the emotion that experience induced. And it does so by playing with language, or by letting a few words have their heads in a play of meaning. In writing "Ward's Island" I was lucky. I lay no claim to extraordinary gifts. On the contrary, I know that in comparison with other more fluent, fertile talents, my slow mind plods and stutters. Nevertheless, I believe that when poets are in the "habit" of language—when we're alert and rhythmically fit—then with prayers to patience and luck we can sometimes produce poems that please even us.

And why inhabit, make, inherit poetry?

Oh, it's the shared comedy of the worst
blessed; the sound leading the hand;
a wordlife running from mind to mind
through the washed rooms of the simple senses;
one of those haunted, undefendable, unpoetic
crosses we have to find.

On Louis MacNeice's
"House on a Cliff"

Indoors the tang of a tiny oil lamp. Outdoors
The winking signal on the waste of sea.
Indoors the sound of the wind. Outdoors the wind.
Indoors the locked heart and the lost key.

Outdoors the chill, the void, the siren. Indoors
The strong man pained to find his red blood cools,
While the blind clock grows louder, faster. Outdoors
The silent moon, the garrulous tides she rules.

Indoors ancestral curse-cum-blessing. Outdoors
The empty bowl of heaven, the empty deep.
Indoors a purposeful man who talks at cross
Purposes, to himself, in a broken sleep.

Louis MacNeice (1907–63) was almost universally beloved by his peers among the English poets, though he was an Irishman from Ulster who fits into none of the categories retrospectively conferred upon his generation. His clergyman father, with roots in the West of Ireland, rose in the Protestant Church of Ireland to become a bishop. Louis was educated in classics at two famous English public schools, adopting at an early age the pose of an atheistical, rather coolly aesthetic bohemian. At Oxford, MacNeice relished the role of a maverick eccentric. He knew, but was junior to, Auden and Spender, and although he later associated with the pro-Communist, pro-Republican intellectuals of the 1930s—on two occasions visiting Spain—an unfinished autobiography published after his death *(The Strings Are False)* shows him to have been, on the whole, a modern stoic, skeptically detached from politics and wittily scornful of simplistic dogma.

As is true of many poets, public and private personae were dissociated in MacNeice, the one built up fancifully, one sup-

From *Touchstones: American Poets on a Favorite Poem,* ed. Robert Pack and Jay Parini (Hanover, NH: University Press of New England, 1996). Reprinted with permission.

poses, to protect the other. Tom Paulin, in an interesting essay,* describes him as an Irishman "from no part," drawing attention to the "anguished sense of displacement that is so fundamental to his imagination." It was not that MacNeice was socially rejected or disliked. Manifestly, he could at will charm his way into any group that attracted him. It was more (or so it appears) that his loneliness was intensely personal, perhaps even self-induced, and that his sharp intelligence restrained him from adopting wholesale ideologies to staunch some incurable yet poetically indispensable wound.

"House on a Cliff," written in 1955, may, as Tom Paulin suggests, metaphorically indicate Ireland, or the ambiguous role that divided nation played in the poet's private history. The poem speaks to me, however, almost entirely of a divided sense of being. Notice, though, how often the words "indoors" and "outdoors" appear in the same line, suggesting that they are extremes of the same spectrum. The "house," more symbol than actuality, is nonetheless "there," a real house where a man has to live, confronted indoors and outdoors with his lonely condition in an indifferent cosmos.

The first three lines call attention to all five senses: the "tang" of the oil lamp, both smelled and tasted; the visible "winking signal" at sea; then the sound of the wind indoors as compared to the feel or touch of the wind outside. This emphasis on immediate sensation is brought about by a syntactical, surely deliberate, omission of verbs; indeed, no copulative verb appears anywhere in the poem. The nouns succeed each other disjointedly, arhythmically, here and there colored by a lopped participle. In the arresting fourth line, two participial phrases, "locked heart" and "lost key," signal an abrupt drop into another register. The lonely house becomes metaphorically the soul, and the two images together throw their long shadows forward, as it were, over a tightening panic.

Though house and sea still preside in the second stanza, the word "siren" (ambiguously warning and enticing) introduces an urban scream, a wail of urgency juxtaposed with the ticking of

*Tom Paulin, "The Man from No Part: Louis MacNeice," in *Ireland and the English Crisis* (Newcastle upon Tyne: Bloodaxe Books, 1984), 75–79.

the "blind clock" (a characteristic MacNeicean image) sugges-
tive both of "blind" mechanical time and the helpless aging of a
beating heart. Again, a jagged enjambment "Outdoors" at the
end of the third line leads to a renewed image of the sea—ruled
by the (contrastingly) "silent" and timeless moon. Surprisingly
(or maybe not surprisingly), the moon in this mechanical uni-
verse remains a "she": "the garrulous tides she rules." Both per-
sonifications may appear inappropriate to the ahuman empti-
ness of "outdoors"—unless the she-ness of the moon represents
a threat to the he-ness of the speaker. One doesn't know how
conscious or unconscious MacNeice was of this "slip."

MacNeice was surely conscious, though, of the explicit nihil-
ism that "outdoors" brings to the final stanza: "the empty [God-
less] bowl of heaven, the empty deep." In the face of which the
"purposeful [intellectual] man" caught helplessly in the "ances-
tral curse-cum-blessing" of his inheritance, "talks at cross / Pur-
poses, to himself, in a broken sleep." The repercussions of that
"cross" at the end of the penultimate line are extraordinarily
resonant. *Cross* suggests anger, of course, and impotence (crossed
wires that defeat attempts at communication with others) while at
the same time symbolizing the Christian cross (which MacNeice
had abandoned, not without guilt) together with all the other
implications that being "crossed" or importantly frustrated bring
to mind. There is also a sense in which the entire poem is a "cross"
between the stressed meters of English and the quantitative me-
ters of Greek and Latin, a cross that makes for restlessness and
rhythmic tension in nearly all MacNeice's work.

I think I have said enough to show that this seemingly simple
English lyric, sealed in traditional stanzas and rhymes, is in fact a
work of mysterious, dreamlike profundity. *The Strings Are False*
records a number of MacNeice's dreams, and "House on a Cliff"
may well be oneiric in origin. Yet the surrealism of its imagery,
like the "nihilism" of its message, is so brilliantly confounded by
the compressed passion and puissance of its form, that a reader
is drawn into the spell before he begins to search for meanings.

The Uses of Prytherch

The Early Poetry of R. S. Thomas

Once upon a time, on a gusty, wet afternoon in November, a young American mother parked her pram and sleeping baby in the lobby of the Hammersmith Public Library and guiltily ducked inside. She was looking for a book of poems. At her American university, before marrying in England, she had studied with passion the poetry of Herbert and Donne, Frost, Yeats and Eliot. Now England (not, alas, Bloomsbury) and marriage (not out of Jane Austen) had pretty well driven poetry out of her life. Foundering, bewildered, cold, not very happy, she was seeking the poems of a famous Welshman, not long dead, called Dylan Thomas. I can still see her forefinger traveling along the celluloid-covered titles on the poetry shelf: Auden, Bridges, Eliot, Hopkins, Muir—ah, Thomas. But the book she pulled out (a stone wall depicted on the binding) was not by the anticipated Dylan; it was the work of a poet she had never heard of: *Song at the Year's Turning,* by R. S. Thomas.

On the point of returning the volume to the shelf, she leafed through it. An introduction by John Betjeman warmly recommended the work of a country parson whose appeal went "beyond the Welsh border." R. S. Thomas was evidently another Welsh poet who wrote in English. It was impressive, though, that he had learned the Welsh language to help him understand "the remote hill people" among whom he lived. He was a nature poet, too, without the stigma of being Georgian or neo-Georgian. His feeling for Wales and Welsh dissent had enabled him to identify with the minister of his narrative poem . . . and so on. All this sounded strange enough to that young American. (She has since come to realize how little Betjeman comprehended—despite the generosity of his recommendation—of R. S. Thomas's complicated conscience; or of the Wales in which is rooted his prolonged quarrel with himself.)

From *The Page's Drift: R. S. Thomas at Eighty,* ed. M. Wynn Thomas (Bridgend, Wales: Seren Books, 1993). Also published in *New England Review* 15, no. 4 (fall 1993). Reprinted with permission.

Nevertheless, opening the book at random, she read to the end a poem called "Affinity."

> Consider this man in the field beneath,
> Gaitered with mud, lost in his own breath,
> Without joy, without sorrow,
> Without children, without wife,
> Stumbling insensitively from furrow to furrow,
> A vague somnambulist; but hold your tears,
> For his name also is written in the Book of Life.
>
> (*SYT*, 25)*

Simple lines, but masterly. The rhymes and half-rhymes, enviably smooth, guided the sense through the stanza with none of the exhibitionist bravura of that other Thomas so familiar to Americans like my apprentice self—for why pretend any longer that bewildered young mother was anyone else? Especially striking was the way the line-beat varied, from two stresses in the generally anapestic "Without joy, without sorrow, / Without children, without wife" to five or six stresses in the last: "For his name also is written in the Book of Life."

English prosody has yet to evolve a notation that can represent the subtleties of phrase and rhythm in poetry like this. Anyone with an ear will unconsciously register the pattern of stresses, light syllables, and pauses that in each line combine to achieve unostentatious wholeness. What the poem *says* is inseparable from what it *is*. A tone of moral injunction secures itself in the diction, yet every time a line veers toward rhetoric, the taut verse intervenes and pulls it back into the immediacy of the poem's occasion. If, for example, the rhymed couplet in the middle of the second stanza verges on preachiness, the sequel carries the verse into the realm of vision.

> From the standpoint of education or caste or creed
> Is there anything to show that your essential need
> Is less than his, who has the world for church,
> And stands bare-headed in the woods' wide porch
> Morning and evening to hear God's choir
> Scatter their praises?

---

*See p. 153 for list of abbreviations.

Again, if "God's choir" edges toward bathos, the effect is soon dissipated by the right-thereness of

> Don't be taken in
> By stinking garments or an aimless grin.

So it was that on a dark English day thirty-five years ago, this poem—not one Thomas chose to reprint in later collections—revealed itself to me instantly as the real thing: clear, closely knit, spare, and forceful by reason of its appropriate form. How much of this I understood at the time I don't know. After I had read "Affinity" and the lovely translation from the Welsh, "Night and Morning," on the facing page, I checked out Thomas's book and, with my crying baby and bulky shopping, returned home to read it.

In part, my reason for attempting an essay on work that R. S. Thomas may by now reject or regret having published is to thank this poet whose fastidious ear and assured command of English verse brought poetry back to me—or me to poetry—in a bleak time of my youth. *Song at the Year's Turning* has remained a touchstone through the years. It seems important to emphasize that it was (and is) Thomas's *poetry* that impressed me; not only his fine technique, but the passion that seemed to well up from within it. That the passion was Welsh and its expression English can be seen today as the source of harrowing tension. But that was not so conspicuous then.

In "The Making of a Poem," a talk given in 1969, Thomas himself declared, "One of my objections to . . . reviewers and columnists is that they . . . nearly always go over what [my] poems are about . . . the hill country of Wales; the Welsh political and social existence; the natural world; the struggle between time and eternity; the struggle between reason and the emotions." While Thomas readily admits, in this lecture to librarians, that he himself may be responsible for such reviews because he "pushes" his ideas at people, still, he says, this "is not what a poet should do at all." He goes on to explain that poetry, for him, as for all poets deserving of the name, "is a matter of technique" (*Prose,* 109).

> If a poet realises that it has been his privilege to have a certain gift in the manipulation of language . . . then he is obviously

committed from the very beginning to a lifetime of self disci-
pline, struggle, disappointment, failure with just possibly that
odd success which is greater in his eyes than it probably is in the
eyes of anybody else. (*Prose*, 111)

Later on in the same passage, Thomas adds, in a characteris-
tic tone of self-questioning, "there must be some kind of music
which one is after, and indeed isn't this what makes poetry
memorable? Isn't it just the way of saying things which really is
part of our appreciation of poetry, and the thing that makes
poetry last through the centuries?"

It is pertinent to keep those remarks on technique and music
in mind while considering the overall direction and develop-
ment of Thomas's poems over twenty-five years; roughly, from
1942, when he became rector of Manafon in the border county of
Montgomeryshire, to 1967, when he left Eglwys-fach, south of the
Dyfi estuary, and moved further west and north to Aberdaron on
Welsh-speaking Llŷn. His geographical migration parallels the
thematic configuration of his poetry; and both manifest a con-
scious and deliberate withdrawal from England (including the
forms of English verse) and a correspondingly self-monitored
identification with Wales and Welsh culture. In Aberdaron, after
the publication of *Not That He Brought Flowers* in 1968, he severely
winnowed his earlier work, dropping from the six (really nine)
collections represented in his *Selected Poems, 1946–1968* many
poems that his readers knew well and must have expected to find.
Why? Why, in the early 1970s, did he discard from this retrospec-
tive volume good poems that recorded step by step the process of
a spiritual and mental dialectic that for twenty-five years had
empowered his verse? Can a shape or paradigm be found in the
early books that will shed light on the direction of the later ones?

Thomas's "early" poems—Thomas was forty-two when *Song at the
Year's Turning* was published (1955); two years older than
George Herbert when he died—are sometimes known as the
"Prytherch poems" after Iago Prytherch, a name the poet "jest-
ingly" invented for a hill-farmer he once saw docking mangles
while "visiting a 1,000 feet up farm in Manafon."[1] The name
Iago Prytherch, strange to English ears, is common enough in
Welsh. Iago simply means James, pronounced with a short *a*, as

in "baggage" or "map"; it bears no relation, probably, to the long-*æ*d villain of *Othello*. Prytherch, or Prydderch in Welsh, would be a contraction of ap Rhydderch, or son of Rhytherch. It is not likely that "Prytherch" has significance as a name, apart from its being a Welsh surname given to an English-speaking hill-farmer, rooting him in Wales and its hereditary Celtic tree.[2] When he first appears in "A Peasant," Iago Prytherch more or less merges with other, often unnamed men of the soil and mixen: "Just an ordinary man of the bald Welsh hills, / Who pens a few sheep in a gap of cloud." Like Davies who died "with his face to the wall . . . in his stone croft" (*SYT*, 59), like Twm of "The Airy Tomb," Prytherch represents an amalgam of laborers and poor farmers in *The Stones of the Field* and *An Acre of Land* who "compelled" the poet's gaze.

It has long been apparent, though, that Iago Prytherch, perhaps "real" to begin with, through the years came to represent a good deal more than a rural type. Writing on the Prytherch poems in 1971, H. J. Savill confirmed what is surely plain to anyone who reads them in sequence: that Prytherch evolved to become a conscience or alter ego for Thomas; as Savill puts it, "a control, a sounding board for the poet's personal sense of conflict."[3]

Thomas himself has recorded, in Welsh prose, how, upon arriving in Manafon, his parish of materialistic border-Welsh hill-farmers at first shocked and repelled him. "Manafon was an eye-opener to me," he said in the radio talk "Y Llwybrau Gynt" in 1972.

Here I became aware of the clash between dream and reality. I was a proper little bourgeois, brought up delicately, with the mark of the church and the library on me. I had seen this part of the country from the train in the evening through a romantic haze. I now found myself among hard, materialistic, industrious people, who measured each other in acres and pounds; Welshmen who turned their backs on their inheritance. . . ; farmers of the cold, bare hillsides, who dreamed of saving enough money to move to a more fertile farm on the plains. (*Prose*, 138)

The conflicts that resulted in the Manafon poems were born, surely, of that first confrontation with the "real world." The "clash between dream and reality"—the same that beset Yeats in Ireland—would seem to set the younger Thomas, too, in the mainstream of the late Romantic tradition. His self-doubt ("a proper little bourgeois") bespeaks disdain for his own intellectual status ("the mark of the church and the library"). At the same time, the poet was disturbed by the crudeness and materialism of the hill-farmers, in whom he had hoped to find a "magical and mysterious" Welshness he had not found in a previous parish on the plains of Flintshire (*Prose*, 138).[4]

How Thomas responded and dealt with romantic disillusion is hinted at in his prose, although one has to read poems such as "Memories" (*SYT*, 45) to realize how, when romantic fantasy gave way to a sense of reality, he tried on alternative Romantic ideas, conspicuously those developed in the early nineteenth century by Coleridge and Wordsworth. In Manafon, Thomas's imagination abandoned the "magical and mysterious" and instead looked hard at the place where he was. He remained, however reluctantly (or so it seems to me), a precarious and increasingly self-conscious, self-critical Romantic. Ned Thomas, in an essay introducing the *Selected Prose*, writes convincingly of what he calls R. S. Thomas's "clash of Romanticisms"; for example, "The late Romanticism of the far horizon that was so often projected onto the Celtic West is rejected but in its place appears a new and fresh Romanticism, grounded in *this* place and welling up in the heart in the manner of the great early Romantics" (*Prose*, 9). The essay goes on to associate Thomas's evolving outlook not only with the German and English movement of the nineteenth century but, to a limited extent, with a Welsh-language tradition nearer at hand in the work of his contemporary Waldo Williams (*Prose*, 11).

Whatever Thomas may believe about Romanticism, his writing repeatedly insists that the feelings "welling up in his heart" in Manafon radically affected the tenor of his ideas and the dilemmas those ideas brought to his poetry.[5] The passage from "Y Llwybrau Gynt" quoted above continues,

[Manafon] was in some ways an old-fashioned district. When I went there in 1942, there was not a single tractor in the area. The men worked with their hands, hoeing, sheep-shearing, collecting hay, and cutting hedges. The horse was still in use. There was a smithy there; I can hear the sound of the anvil still, and see the sparks flying. I can remember the lonely figures in the fields, hoeing or docking mangles, hour after hour. What was going on in their heads, I wonder? The question remains unanswered to this day. (*Prose*, 138–39)

Such recollections, exact, moving, tinged slightly with nostalgia, provide no evidence that Thomas came to know or understand his hill-farmers. On the contrary, as he repeatedly lamented in poetry and prose, their existence seemed inconceivably distant from his own. It was, surely, the gnawing bafflement and pity he felt when faced with people like Prytherch that set him writing. When the dream was lost, responsibilities to other ideals began to emerge. If the Wales he loved, with its birds and trees and mountains, was also a nation of "old fashioned ways" and inarticulate farmers, then the poet would have to forge links with them, as with their "cold, bare hillsides" and the Welsh language they had forgotten. Confronting what he saw as insensibility in his rural parishioners, he contemplated them—the conundrum of their minds and the harsh realities of their lives—with a view not so much of teaching them as of learning from them how to approach himself. If he could not show them how to value what they, as Welshmen, so preciously possessed, could he himself believe in that idyll—so dear to him—of a shared inheritance: cultural, natural, Christian, and national? In the context of his ideal, "What was going on in their heads, I wonder?" became absolutely pivotal to the prolonged self-interrogation that sustains the dramatic tension in Thomas's first five or six books.[6]

As Thomas set it up for himself, the dispute with the farmers of Montgomeryshire (i.e., with his own ideas) that pervades *Song at the Year's Turning* and continues to break out in *Poetry for Supper, Tares,* and *The Bread of Truth* was bound to result in the poet's seeming defeat. (If it had been a real defeat, Thomas would not have gone on writing.) "All in vain. I will cease now / My long absorption with the plough," Thomas declares in "No Through Road," the last poem in *Song at the Year's Turning.*

> I have failed after many seasons
> To bring truth to birth,
> And nature's simple equations
> In the mind's precincts do not apply.

This acknowledgment of failure, though, is tantamount to a statement of purpose: the poet has tried, he says, *(a)* to lay bare the truth in art, and *(b)* to reconcile nature's rules, or "simple equations," with the complex mind that creates poetry. In confessing that such connections can't be made, he shows, in the following stanza, that they *must.* "But where to turn?" He answers himself immediately by returning to "nature," even as he despairs of representing it in language.

> Earth endures
> After the passing, necessary shame
> Of winter, and the old lie
> Of green places beckons me still
> From the new world, ugly and evil,
> That men pry for in truth's name.

More forbidding than anything in nature is the "new world" that science and technology are bringing about in the name of truth: notice that men now "pry" for it; that is, no longer pray. The "old lie," for Thomas, is preferable to the new truth. One sees here that the argument has veered away from the puzzle of Prytherch and other men of the soil. It seems now to take place in the pained consciousness of a man who, having got rid of his Romantic, idealized illusions, faces with horror the intolerable condition of the world without them.

The apparent finality of "No Through Road" is really, then, a point of new departure: the poet, now allied with Prytherch, stands in opposition to the "evil" mechanizing treads of contemporary culture. This poem's place, moreover, at the end of Thomas's first selection seems to inform us that a chapter of the poet's mental traveling is over.

It is helpful, I think, to regard each of Thomas's books as a lap in a personal journey—a quest that seems bound to fail because it seeks a truth that, on one hand, cannot be logical or proved by reason, but on the other, has to be "proved" against the Romantic lie. A map or graph can be imagined that would chart the contradictions and temptations this poet forced himself to overcome as he persevered on his barefoot way. His books, of course, overlap; and the line (or maze) that connects them is continuous. Nevertheless, there are halting places, pits of despair, a few dazzling peaks of arrival, interspersed with shifts or changes in the overall topography. These latter tend to occur after a subject has worn itself out, working through every possible cranny of the poet's consciousness.

Such a subject was Prytherch and his brothers of the Montgomeryshire hills. *Song at the Year's Turning* did not, in fact, exhaust Thomas's "long absorption with the plough," although at least thirty of its sixty-three lyrics dwell on the enigma of unthinking laboring man. When Prytherch returns in subsequent collections, it is to a somewhat less solidly earthed, more metaphysical and defensive context. Up to 1955 or so, the figure of Prytherch invited, over and over, the same amazed gaze of revulsion and fascination, followed usually by self-castigation and a humbled acknowledgment of his status as a man. The struggle was never one, however, in which the laborer participated; it occurred within the mind of the poet even when, as in "Invasion on the Farm," Prytherch himself was given an anxious, protesting monologue.

> I am Prytherch. Forgive me. I don't know
> What you are talking about; your thoughts flow
> Too swiftly for me.

(SYT, 102)

The farmworkers described in the more typical "A Peasant" and "Affinity" are spoken *about,* but have nothing to say for themselves. "Blind? Yes, and deaf and dumb, and the last irks most," cries the speaker in "Enigma" (*SYT*, 68). Repeatedly the peasant is seen to be rooted in the land, more plant than man, "enduring like a tree under the curious stars" ("A Peasant," *SYT*, 21); or as one who pulls "the reluctant swedes" until "his back comes straight / Like an old tree lightened of the snow's weight" ("A Labourer," *SYT*, 18). In *An Acre of Land*, the same laborer, or one identical to him, is seen as "A wild tree still, whose seasons are not yours" ("The Labourer," *SYT*, 70).

As Ned Thomas demonstrates (*Prose*, 11–12), the tree is an image or emblem that weaves through all Thomas's work. Converging with the image of the fountain,[7] it knits up the apparent contradictions, again and again appearing as a symbol of endurance, of hope, of nature, of poetry "that is eternity wearing / the green leaves of time" ("Prayer"). It is in terms of a tree, finally, that Prytherch gains his victory over the world and the poet alike.

> Power, farmer? It was always yours.
> Not the new physics' terrible threat
> To the world's axle, nor the mind's subtler
> Manipulation of our debt
>
> To nature: but an old gift
> For weathering the slow recoil
> Of empires with a tree's patience,
> Rooted in the dark soil.
>
> ("Iago Prytherch," *PS*, 37)

Open, almost anywhere, any of Thomas's books published before 1961 to find Prytherch or Prytherch's double, described as a creature more of nature than of humanity, rooted in the land, sometimes sensitive to his surroundings, "your soul made strong by the earth's incense" ("Absolution," *PS*, 44), sometimes "Wasting his frame under the ripped coat / ... Contributing grimly to the accepted pattern, / the embryo music dead in his throat" ("The Welsh Hill Country," *SYT*, 46). Yet a penetrating reading shows us such figures, not only *as* trees, rooted in the soil, but as potential inheritors of the one "great tree" that is Wales: "Its roots were nourished with their blood" ("The Tree: *Owain Glyn Dwr Speaks*," *SYT*, 56–58). This heraldic tree of Welsh legend, together with the Christian tree that is the cross, is invoked often enough in the early poems to offset the bitterness of their realism with a lyrical, even mystical, iconography.

> He kneeled long,
> And saw love in a dark crown
> Of thorns blazing, and a winter tree
> Golden with fruit of a man's body.
>
> ("In a Country Church," *SYT*, 114)

As early as 1946, after the publication of *The Stones of the Field*, Thomas was being attacked by fellow Welshmen for the grimness of his rural portraits. Pennar Davies, in a broadcast on November 21 of that year, commented, "R. S. Thomas sees far more uncouthness in the men of the Welsh hills than I have ever been able to detect."[8] Such criticism is understandable. With the spread of Nonconformity through Wales, "a yawning gulf," in the words of the historian Kenneth O. Morgan, "opened up between the anglicized gentry and the . . . Welsh-speaking majority." Welsh culture "emerged from below, from the tenant farmers and labourers on their smallholdings."[9] The extension of the franchise and the reform of local government in the late nineteenth century, with the great transfer of landownership before and after the First World War, made these farmers masters of their own land. The Welsh tradition they inherited, founded on the Nonconformism that had saved their language and culture, was one in which education, poetry, and music were cherished. In his (Welsh) poem "Ffermwr Rhyddfrydol" (Liberal farmer) Bobi Jones—a younger contemporary of R. S. Thomas—brings one such farmer vividly to life: "He was so stout: but when he spoke his pure harsh consonants / I felt like an exile on a distant continent / Hearing through bars the forgotten echo / Of the language of his boots."[10] Even before the advent of tractors and electricity, Bobi Jones's "stout farmer" would scarcely have recognized himself in Iago Prytherch. But, of course, Prytherch, almost from the beginning, was a projection of an idea; a partner in a purely internal dialogue.

Moreover, as H. J. Savill points out, Thomas's farmers and laborers did not belong to Welsh-speaking Wales. They were, in Thomas's eyes, impoverished English-speaking border people, indifferent to the Welshness that he desired to restore to them. Importantly for Thomas, too, they were a people left out by advancing civilization and, therefore, through their very backwardness and ignorance salvageable as representatives of an "old world" everywhere threatened by the "evil" new one.

It is not surprising, either, that Thomas, who was born and educated outside the Welsh cultural tradition, looked at Prytherch and his kind and saw there a curious affinity; both he and they were anomalies in Wales. His disgust with himself and his background could be transferred to them, and shared. That the Anglican priest was articulate and the hill-farmers mute meant that, in reaching out to them, he could try to speak for them. And yet, paradoxically, this poet's romantic vision gave him to understand that education and articulation (especially in English) were themselves a form of corruption.

So it was that Thomas found himself torn between revulsion at the passive insensitivity of his hill-farmers and admiration (eventually reverence) for the strength of their innocence. The tension bore fruit in all the poetry of the Prytherch period.

Part of the paradox of Thomas's position in Manafon was that he represented the recently disestablished Anglican Church of Wales. Welsh-speaking farmers would have attended a Non-conformist Baptist, Presbyterian, or Methodist chapel. In "The Minister" Thomas lambasts the Calvinism preached by Elias Morgan.

> Protestantism—the adroit castrator
> Of art; the bitter negation
> Of song and dance and the heart's innocent joy—
> You have botched our flesh and left us only the soul's
> Terrible impotence in a warm world.
>
> (*SYT*, 92)

In "Dau Gapel" (1948), however, Thomas wrote of Noncon-formism with enthusiasm: "Speaking of denominations, I must admit that Nonconformity wins hands down. . . . The Church of Wales isn't any longer Welsh enough in spirit" (*Prose*, 46–47). Here was another source of contradiction for the Anglican priest and artist struggling to come to terms with the "truth," with the farmers who were his parishioners and with the Wales he associated with spiritual wholeness.

A poem that seems central to the tangle of conflicts that runs right through *Song at the Year's Turning* is one called "A Priest to His People" (*SYT*, 27). It is not as dramatically affecting as "The Minister," but it is typical of Thomas's struggle at the time. The huge swing of its dialectic, from harangue to celebration, with its uneasy resolution in baffled submission is like a blueprint of this period's (productive) continuing battle. The poem begins brutally.

> Men of the hills, wantoners, men of Wales
> With your sheep and your pigs and your ponies, your sweaty
>   females,
> How I have hated you for your irreverence, your scorn even
> Of the refinements of art and the mysteries of the Church.

"Hated" is a strong word; "sweaty females" is shocking. But notice how Thomas puts the priest in a false position he is *bound* to forfeit. Hatred, disgust, arrogance—such powerfully un-Christian feelings are spat out in an invective of self-defense. Protecting the "refinements" of his tastes, the speaker is ignoring the earth of his origin. The "men of bone" he addresses, "who have not yet shaken the moss from [their] savage skulls," detect his falseness: the priest's "true heart" is "wandering in a wood of lies." And what are these lies? The forms of the Church, "the pale words in the black book" offered so unprofitably to people "whose hands can dabble in the world's blood." Equally suspect are the forms of art.

> I have taxed your ignorance of rhyme and sonnet.
> Your want of deference to the painter's skill,
> But I know, as I listen, that your speech has in it
> The source of all poetry, clear as a rill
> Bubbling from your lips.

Today Thomas would almost certainly reject such lines—cleverly rhymed, rhythmical, conventionally Romantic in sentiment. Implied is a criticism of all that culture stands for, couched in "poetic" English that he now bitterly stands against. In the 1940s, when *Stones of the Field* was being written, Thomas was still attracted by the pastoral ideal. Nonetheless, the priest soon sees how "indifferent they are to all I can offer, / Caring not whether I blame or praise." This is where Thomas, of course, departs from the traditional model. Pastoral encomiums will not satisfy the "truth." In the end, priest and people remain irremediably separated, the priest locked within his Church of "refinements" and "mysteries," the people unaware that "higher" sentiments exist.

> With your pigs and your sheep and your sons and holly-cheeked
>   daughters
> You will still continue to unwind your days
> In a crude tapestry under the jealous heavens
> To affront, bewilder, yet compel my gaze.

A theme common to the poems of *Song at the Year's Turning* can be identified as intense Romantic longing, frustrated by the poet's faithfulness to the truth he perceives. His defeat at the hands of reality is paradoxically a victory for the "failure" he unearths, after he has cast away his false illusions. The question arises, how much of his residual, hard-won insight is true, how much still false? Determined to be scrupulously honest, conditioning himself by renouncing the lyrical pulse that thrust him into poetry in the first place, Thomas set out, it appears, in pursuit of a metaphysic that would supersede his endemic intellectuality by giving him access to some holy unity of body and spirit, earth and mind, that he glimpsed only at moments. Such a longed-for state of exalted reality became for Thomas the uncertain promise that sanctified his quest—Wordsworth's "central peace subsisting at the heart / of endless agitation," Eliot's "still point of the turning world."

Keeping such an elusive, essential possibility alive—while the dialogue with Prytherch rumbled on—meant that a number of intermediate poems, written along the way, as it were, had to be pruned once they had served their purpose. Of the eighteen published poems in which Prytherch appears,[11] Thomas preserved only three for his *Selected Poems:* "A Peasant," which first introduced him (it also introduces the selection and is its point of departure); "Invasion on the Farm," which reverses the roles of poet and persona, allowing Prytherch to voice his misgivings under threat from the poet's challenge; and finally, some late consolations of philosophy offered by the poet to the laborer in a curt "Aside."

> Take heart, Prytherch.
> Over you the planets stand,
> And have seen more ills than yours.
> This canker was in the bone
> Before man bent to his image
> In the pool's glass. Violence has been
> And will be again. Between better
> And worse is no bad place
>
> For a labourer, whose lot is to seem
> Stationary in traffic so fast.
> Turn aside, I said; do not turn back.
> There is no forward and no back
> In the fields, only the year's two
> Solstices, and patience between.

(*SP*, 91)

"Aside" partakes of the self-searchings and assertions of *Pietà*, in which it appeared in 1966. At once didactic and resigned, it signals an end to the long question and answer of the Prytherch debate, and may have seemed to Thomas the most satisfying of his attempts finally to reconcile the outlooks of priest and peasant. Between "A Peasant" and "Aside," some of the best of Prytherch has been lost ("The Gap in the Hedge" [*SYT*, 53] for instance, with its haunting ambiguity) along with weaker chapters in the story: the nostalgic, somewhat patronizing "Memories" (*SYT*, 45), the almost melodramatic "Temptation of a Poet" (*PS*, 14), the embittered "Too Late" (*T*, 25). None of the shifts in attitude explored in *Poetry for Supper* appear in the *Selected Poems*, although the former book, with *Tares*, traces Prytherch's metamorphosis from a mute toiler in the fields to a "scholar of the soil" who is seen to have been "right the whole time" ("Absolution," *PS*, 44), and is now chiefly threatened, not by the poet who loves him, but by modern methods of farming "That will destroy you and your race" ("Too Late," *T*, 25).

By the time *Tares* appeared in 1961, Prytherch was clearly a type Thomas honored and wished to preserve in Wales, but his symbolic presence was not so urgently relied on. The Nonconformist farmer Walter Llywarch (*SP*, 60), describing his isolated life in a Welsh valley, delivers a cool monologue of defeat that has little to do with the poet's metaphysical conflict. Likewise "On the Farm" (*SP*, 82) departs from the Prytherch pattern, presenting the "no good" Pew family objectively, in grim ironical stanzas that, at the end, plunge into dark hints of corruption.

> And lastly there was the girl:
> Beauty under some spell of the beast.
> Her pale face was the lantern
> By which they read in life's dark book
> The shrill sentence: God is love.

Poems like this—detached, pared to the bone and technically stunning—rightly, in my opinion, filtered out a good deal of self-questioning and ideological gesturing from the *Selected Poems*. Prytherch is interesting to those who have followed the to-and-fros of Thomas's mental strife, but in the later poems he is better placed behind the scenes. Thomas, it would seem, having sputtered at his critics and openly explained his relationship to Prytherch in "Iago Prytherch" (*PS*, 36) while beseeching him for forgiveness (see also "Absolution," *PS*, 44) at last felt ready to release him. "Servant," from the *Bread of Truth* says as much, providing the title of that collection in its last line.

> You served me well, Prytherch.
> From all my questioning and doubts;
> From brief acceptance of the times'
> Deities; from ache of the mind
> Or body's tyranny, I turned . . .
> To where you read in the slow book
> Of the farm, turning the fields' pages . . .
> . . . proving in your bone and in your blood
> Its accuracy.

Prytherch had not, of course, given "the whole answer." The poem goes on to balance the equation.

> Is truth so bare,
> So dark, so dumb, as on your hearth
> And in your company I found it?
> Is not the evolving print of the sky
> To be read, too; the mineral
> Of the mind worked?

The poet, given his eye for beauty and his capacity for working "the mineral of the mind," can choose a "higher" truth "With a clear eye and free hand / From life's bounty." Prytherch has no such advantage.

> Not choice for you,
> But seed sown upon the thin
> Soil of a heart, not rich, nor fertile,
> Yet capable of the one crop.
> Which is the bread of truth I break.
>
> (*BT*, 41)

As R. S. Thomas increasingly abandoned the prosodic models of English verse and secured his poetry in a voice that drew strength from conceptual imagery ("evolving print of the sky"; "mineral of the mind"), certain ideas he found himself promoting—such as "higher" truth for the educated and plain "bread of truth" for Prytherch—may well have distressed him. Poems like "Servant" made the conflict between beauty and truth seem more, rather than less, insoluble. Even to call Prytherch a "servant" seems to relegate the values he represents to a lesser status: and this was not, I believe, what Thomas intended to do. The dialectic of assertion, withdrawal, and pained reconsideration that characterizes the Prytherch poems seeks, surely, to represent Prytherch and priest as equals. The chasm they are asked to bridge lies between nature's truth and the ideas educated people formulate in language in order to comprehend and communicate. Yet language, to Thomas (as to Wittgenstein and subsequent linguistic philosophers of the twentieth century) is not in the end capable of bridging the gap between reality and itself. This state of affairs is plainly set forth in "Epitaph."

> The poem in the rock and
> The poem in the mind
> Are not one.
> It was in dying
> I tried to make them so.
>
> (*PS*, 48)

How is a reader to take such a poem's despairing assertion? As resignation? As a threat? Or as the stripped bedrock on which to found new attempts to build truth out of language? It appears that at a stage in his progress, Thomas was willing to "die," or in the words of his essay, to "commit suicide" as a poet,[12] in order to marry the irreconcilable concepts of intellect and instinct, body and mind, language and reality. As he must have seen, when he attempted synthesis by argument or plain assertion, he failed to convince himself. He seems to have "said" things in his poems in order to prove himself wrong. It was by airing his arguments that he discovered where he was mistaken. The poem he called "Green Categories" (*PS*, 19), in which he confronts Prytherch with Kant, is a case in point.[13] However, it appears that Thomas often *did* succeed in satisfying himself when, exhausted by mental strife, he dropped naturally into images. "Don't think, look!" Wittgenstein advised, after anguished years of fighting the antinomies Kant categorically forced into partnership.[14]

As a poet, though, Thomas has the advantage over the philosophers. For where philosophy, of its very nature, has to expound abstract ideas, poetry is like painting; it talks with images. Like music, too, it is a "language" of sound. To be art, of course, images and sound have to communicate through a logic of their own. Yet the vital ambiguity and multiple resonances of imagistic expression give the poet a chance.

In "Absolution" (*PS*, 42), Thomas grants to Prytherch a patient wisdom denied to the poet, but he still reserves to himself the intelligence that finds this out. The very acknowledgment "It was you who were right" opens a loophole through which the poet can escape into a field of "things," that is, *away* from his ideas. He cannot become a Prytherch, docking mangels in the dusk, but he knows now where he fell into error: "I have worn my soul bare / On the world's roads, seeking what lay / Too close for *the mind's lenses to see*" (my italics). Seeing, then, offers the poet salvation, and it is, after all, Prytherch who has shown him how to look.

When, in the first poem of *Tares*, Thomas sets forth his compassionate reasons for making Prytherch central to his story, he ignores the infinitely valuable lesson he has been taught in return. "The Dark Well" (*T*, 9) is a poem of conscience; it *tells* us why Prytherch deserves compassion.

> There are two hungers, hunger for bread
> And hunger of the uncouth soul
> For the light's grace. I have seen both,
> And chosen for an indulgent world's
> Ear the story of one whose hands
> Have bruised themselves on the locked doors
> Of life; whose heart, fuller than mine
> Of gulped tears, is the dark well
> From which to draw, drop after drop,
> The terrible poetry of his kind.

To say that, as a poem, "The Dark Well" is overstated (though heartfelt) probably does Thomas an injustice. But as so often, Thomas here asserts, in lines of verse, feelings that he asks his readers to accept as statements. The sentiments are strongly felt, and yes, they are couched in metaphor. Nevertheless, the figurative language is illustrative, and not really intrinsic to the poem.

A quality of exegesis, of sermonizing explanation, "pushes" them (Thomas's own word in "The Making of a Poem") at the reader, and the words speak darkly from the priest's conscience, not from the poet's freedom. For that élan we sometimes call revelation—that outward push from the traps of "truth" and guilt—one has to turn to something like "The Place," with which Thomas chose to end his *Selected Poems*.

> Summer is here.
> Once more the house has its
> Spray of martins, Proust's fountain
> Of small birds, whose light shadows
> Come and go in the sunshine
> Of the lawn as thoughts do
> In the mind.

Poetry happens when image and thought are fired simultaneously by language, compounding idea and vision in an indivisible whole. Toward the end of "The Place" Thomas lets the fountain of martins "build in" himself, and their "bitter migrations" represent his; but the analogy is so delicately drawn that the birds remain in the ascendant—images of renewal and certainty that may well have surprised the poet, as he came joyfully to see them:

> my method is so
> To have them about myself
> Through the hours of this brief
> Season and to fill with their
> Movement, that it is I they build
> In and bring up their young
> To return to after the bitter
> Migrations, knowing the site
> Inviolate through its outward changes.

ABBREVIATIONS

SYT	*Song at the Year's Turning*
PS	*Poetry for Supper*
T	*Tares*
BT	*The Bread of Truth*

NOTES

1. H. J. Savill, "The Iago Prytherch Poems of R. S. Thomas," *Anglo-Welsh Review* 20, no. 45 (1971): 143; reprinted in *Critical Writings on R. S. Thomas,* ed. Sandra Anstey (Bridgend: Poetry Wales Press, 1982), 51. Page references are to *Critical Writings.*

2. The author is grateful to the Welsh poet Dewi Stephen Jones for his comments and translations from the Welsh.

3. Savill, "Iago Prytherch Poems," 53.

4. Writing of himself in the third person in his autobiography, *neb* (nobody), Thomas vividly describes the Manafon he found in 1942: "Manafon scarcely existed. There was no village, only a church, a tavern, a school, and a shop. The farms were spread across the hills as smallholdings mostly, but with the occasional larger farm. The people were anglicized Welsh, with Welsh names and Shropshire accents. They became the subject of his poetry. To him the country and its surroundings were beautiful. He wished to continue to sing poems of praise about them. But how could one reconcile the lives and attitudes of these farmers to [praise]? On a cold, dark day in November, on his way to visit a family living in a farm a thousand feet above sea level, he noticed the farmer's brother out in the field docking mangels. This made a deep impression on him, and when he returned home after the visit he began writing 'A Peasant,' his first poem to face the reality of the scenes before him" (*neb* [Cardiff: Gwasg Gwynedd, 1985], 42, trans. Dewi Stephen Jones).

5. A further passage from *neb:* "Was it because of the hardness of the people and their work, or because of some nicey-nice quality in himself that the tension arose that was to be a part of his spiritual and literary problems for some years to come? . . . After long hours of hard work in all kinds of weather, what was there to do each night after a meal but nod by the fire before they went to bed under the slates? . . . Earth from earth were they; their only interests were the farm, the animals, prices, and the personal lives of their neighbors. The horizons of some of them did not extend beyond the far side of the valley where they lived" (*neb,* 42–43, trans. Dewi Stephen Jones).

6. R. S. Thomas, 'Abercuawg' (1976): "When I began writing I devised a character called Iago Prytherch—an amalgam of some farmers I used to see at work on the Montgomeryshire hillsides. In the opinion of some, he developed into a symbol of something greater.

And yet I had to ask myself whether he was real at all. And there was something else that would worry me as I saw him sweating or shivering hour after hour in the fields: 'What is he thinking about? What's going on inside his skull? And of course there was always the awful possibility that the answer was—'Nothing.' Nothing. What is nothing?" (*Prose*, 159).

7. In 1956 Waldo Williams published his visionary Welsh poem "Mewn Dau Gae" (Between two fields), which contains these lines, seemingly important to Thomas (see also *Prose*, 12):

> Great was the leaping of hearts, after their ice-age.
> The fountains burst up toward heaven, till,
> Falling back, their tears were like leaves of a tree.
> (Trans. Anthony Conran)

8. Savill, "Iago Prytherch Poems," 54.

9. Kenneth O. Morgan, *Rebirth of a Nation: Wales, 1880–1980* (Oxford: Oxford University Press, 1982), 13–27.

10. Quoted in John Emyr, *Bobi Jones: Writers of Wales* (Cardiff: University of Wales Press, 1991), 29–30.

11. H. J. Savill puts the total number of Prytherch poems at eighteen, to include an earlier romantic, "almost euphoric" "Iago Prytherch" that Thomas suppressed after the publication of *Stones of the Field* in 1946. Savill, "Iago Prytherch Poems," 58.

12. R. S. Thomas, "The Creative Writer's Suicide" (1978), *Prose*, 167–74. See also the introduction by Ned Thomas: "The pressures of the modern world which turned R. S. Thomas's Wales into something with a status close to that of pure idea also have an internalized dimension in language itself" (*Prose*, 13). It seems that Thomas was prepared to sacrifice his English lyricism in order to forge a distinctive Anglo-Welsh voice, but he was *not* prepared to give up the English language in poetry, because Welsh was not his mother tongue.

13. "Green Categories" ends with a reference to the conclusion of Kant's *Critique of Practical Reason,* "der berstirnte Himmel uber mir, und das moralische Gesetz in mir." In the final stanza of "Green Categories" Thomas writes: "[Kant's] logic would have failed; your mind, too, / Exposed suddenly to the cold wind / Of genius, faltered. Yet at night together / In your small garden, fenced from the wild moor's / Constant aggression, you could have been at one, / Sharing your faith over a star's blue fire."

14. See Ray Monk, *Ludwig Wittgenstein: The Duty of Genius* (London: Jonathan Cape, 1990).

The Poetry of Dana Gioia

Review of The Gods of Winter

Seeking a precise adjective to describe Dana Gioia's poetry, I
came up with *beautiful*—an epithet twentieth-century criticism
has smeared with suspicion. To speak of "beautiful" poetry with-
out sneering calls for explanation. Yet there was a period in the
1950s when American poetry seemed to be developing in a
beautiful direction. In 1957, Meridian Books in the United
States and Canada published an anthology edited by Donald
Hall, Robert Pack, and Louis Simpson; it was called *New Poets of
England and America,* and it brought to the public's attention a
group of young lyricists who looked to be turning their backs on
modernism. Robert Frost, their patron father or grandfather,
provided an introduction that, today, will strike some people as
heretical. "Overdevelop the social conscience and make us all
social meddlers," he wrote, welcoming a resurgent, happy mar-
riage between poetry and scholarship. "As I often say a thou-
sand, two thousand, colleges, town and gown together in the
little town they make, give us the best audiences poetry ever had
in all this world."

In retrospect, those were the words of an old man whose influ-
ence on American poetry was running into the sands. Hall-Pack-
Simpson's "formalist" anthology gave rise to a counteranthology,
edited by Donald Allen, that, by representing the work of the new
left, sounded the trump for the radical 1960s. The camp war that
resulted—redskins versus palefaces, university "orthodoxy" ver-
sus experimental extremism—raised a good deal of dust that
during the 1970s and 1980s (ironically enough) settled down
finally in the halls of academe—where most American poets of
all camps now find employment. When the history of twentieth-
century American poetry comes to be written, such ironies will
not be lost upon our great-grandchildren.

Meanwhile, poetry in America, weakened by demotic correct-
ness and critical blindness, stands in need of a thorough clean.

From *Poetry Wales* 27, no. 4 (April 1992). Reprinted with permission.

Dana Gioia has appeared at a good moment to attack the job from two sides. His poetry, harkening back to Frost, Richard Wilbur, and Anthony Hecht, is usually constructed in lines and stanzas, or in blank verse with an unmistakably iambic pulse running through it. His criticism radically attacks the system of "creative-writing programs" and academic jobs for poets whose credentials rest on an overvalued reverence for "creativity." (See *Can Poetry Matter* [Saint Paul: Greywolf Press, 1992].)

The Gods of Winter is an important book, if only because it exemplifies Gioia's courageously aesthetic approach to poetry— to its language and rhythms. Fortunately for those of us who agree with him, it is also a good book. His poems are limpid, mellifluous, quotable, and likely to be loved. Clearly, they are rooted in experience and compassion. Nor can their subject matter be dismissed as genteel. Two long poems, "Counting the Children" and "Homecoming," give weight to a volume that might otherwise concede too much to peaceable iambs. Employing dramatic monologue in a specifically American mode (Edgar Lee Masters, Robert Frost, Robert Lowell) "Counting the Children" meditates on "love's austere and lonely offices" in the person of a Chinese accountant called in to audit the estate of a woman whose life has been spent rifling through rubbish bins to save discarded dolls. At the end, Mr. Choi, viewing his sleeping daughter, has a vision of immortality as a destiny for human souls moving backward, not forward, into time.

> I saw beyond my daughter to all children,
> And, though elated, still I felt confused . . .
>
> What if completion comes only in beginnings?
> The naked tree exploding into flower?
> And all our prim assumptions about time
>
> Prove wrong? What if we cannot read the future
> Because our destiny moves back in time,
> And only memory speaks prophetically?

Moral or meditative philosophizing in poetry is often mockingly outlawed by the English intelligentsia, but it rings true in Gioia's vernacular American; "Counting the Children" has to be considered a triumph. Likewise, the psychological insight that plays through "The Homecoming"—a monologue by a murderer who recounts the gruesome story of his childhood—seems a triumph of descriptive narrative.

Other poems are witty ("Money," "Orchestra") or ironical ("News from Nineteen Eighty-Four"), wry ("The Next Poem") or subtly, though effectively, moving. "Planting a Sequoia," an almost impossible poem to write without sentimentality, only touches on the burial of the poet's "first born son . . . brought back to the elements" with the planting of a sapling giant that will stand "when our family is no more, all of his unborn brothers dead . . . / Silently keeping the secret of your birth."

In retrospect, the poetic civil wars of the American 1960s and 1970s look to have been fought with a good deal of blather over nothing very much. Today we read fine, formal poems like Gioia's or Hecht's, and then avant-garde high-jinks, like the "art" poetry produced by Frank O'Hara or John Ashbery, conceding that, at their best, they are branches with a common root. I take it the root is Walt Whitman. Look hard enough at Eliot, Pound, and William Carlos Williams, and that honest common stock can be spotted there, too. Outward forms may violently disagree, but the heartwood of these poets is shared, together with their wryness and eagerness to branch out into speculation once a tangible or visible connection with the world has been established. Metaphysical rootedness in "things" is a quality Dana Gioia shares, too, with Sylvia Plath, Marianne Moore, Elizabeth Bishop, Amy Clampitt; there is nothing sexist about it; and nothing at all that rejects the reality of the world in the name of ideological, aesthetic, or political correctness.

A poem from the recently published *Selected Poems of Frank O'Hara* called "Ode on Causality" contains the lines "and there's the ugliness we seek in vain / through life and long for like a mortuarian Baudelaire." The pivotal word there is not "ugliness" but "seek." American poetry tends to be a poetry that seeks, and whether it seeks ugliness or beauty, the test of its success rests in the appropriate form of its expression. Where there is too much self-consciousness, piety, or strain for novel effect, it fails—as all copybook poetry ultimately fails. In Dana Gioia we have a poet who succeeds without strain. Almost every poem in *The Gods of Winter* fulfills the expectations raised by its form: a poetry of intuitive honesty that penetrates beyond appearances into possible aspects of the truth.

"The Way You Say the World
Is What You Get"

Breathes there a man, with soul so dead,
Who never to himself hath said,
> This is mine own, mine native land!
Whose heart has ne'er within him burn'd,
As home his footsteps he hath turn'd
> From wandering on a foreign strand.

Famous lines, penned by Sir Walter Scott circa 1805, but they beg a question it never would have occurred to me to ask when I left Michigan for England in 1954. Does "native land" necessarily imply a national identity? England, where I happened to have been born, haunted my American childhood. Having read Scott, Dickens, Jane Austen, and George Eliot but comparatively little twentieth-century literature, my image of Great Britain when I left Michigan was still a fantasy. Yet now that Britain really is, in all its overcrowded, polluted, hideous postindustrial reality, my home, it is to America I return with a romantic sense of revisiting the foreign land of childhood.

In speaking today mainly of Wallace Stevens, I hope to show how this poet (whose psychological orientation was highly Romantic) pressed back against reality (Stevens's phrase) not with the purpose of idealizing actual places but rather of creating around them a set of aesthetic loyalties. Stevens's refusal to locate the joys of art anywhere but in individual imagination illustrates, as perhaps no other poet so clearly does, a break with the romantic tradition that took pains to preserve it in a radical style of modernism. Think, comparatively, of Walter Scott, who together with Robert Burns, almost single-handedly forged the romantic image of Scotland that still invites public credulity. Think of Wordsworth, all unknowingly creating a marketable identity for the Lake District in England. Today, Scott's Scotland is tourism's

---

From a lecture on the theme of The Geography of Identity, given at the University of Michigan's Institute for the Humanities, October 1993. From *Michigan Quarterly Review* 34, no. 1 (winter 1995).

Scotland. And no contemporary poet would dream of living within walking distance of Dove Cottage unless he were writing a thesis on the English Romantics or had a job in the Wordsworth Museum. Yet these landscapes that literature has made meaningful (nature imitating art) and commerce has made pay (in two senses) are what most people go to see—and do see and selectively photograph—when they visit Great Britain.

Yes, but what, you may ask, is it *really* like to live in Britain today? Read the English papers or watch television, and you will get the impression that Britain is little more than a loosely cut-up colony of the United States. Its proverbial gentlemanly, class-ridden "identity," you might say, is in disarray under the assault, for good and evil, of multiculturalism. As in the United States, the old sprawling cities, congested with traffic and depressed by unemployment, are breeding grounds for crime. Ten years of Thatcherism have disastrously widened the gulf between rich and poor. Women, claiming rights to work-opportunity and equal pay, are on the march with blacks, homosexuals, environmentalists, animal-rights agitators, and nuclear-power protesters. In short, political Britain, divided on the question of joining Europe, rife with imperial guilt and sensitive about matters of race and gender, pretty well fits the picture Robert Hughes paints of 1990s America in his controversial book *Culture of Complaint*.[1]

Yet in other ways, Britain, though everywhere in the grip of political anxiety, is still the "place" it has been since the last glaciers receded from the highlands ten thousand years ago. In North Wales, where my husband and I spend as much time as we can, the modern, artificial world can seem far away, even though troops of giant pylons carry electricity to the remotest farmhouses, and improved roads bring tourists enough into Snowdonia to keep its mountain-rescue helicopters ear-splittingly on the alert. The raised sedimentary mountains that encircle our cottage in Cwm Nantcol (geologically part of the Harlech Dome) are hundreds of million years old, dating from the same Cambrian era that laid down the Burgess Shale in the Canadian Rockies. In geological time, human history has occurred in a mere split-second—though in Wales, traces of it can be found everywhere. Roman remains are in many places still a visible presence. Over these the Arthurian myths, mixed with tales from the Mabinogian, throw a mythical haze from the Dark Ages. In the late thirteenth century, the Normans under Edward I finally overcame the native Britons (whose tribes gave the Paleozoic rock strata their geological names), and great square Norman castles—Harlech, Caernarfon, Conwy, Beaumaris—still grandly watch over the empty harbors. And though today most Welsh-speakers are patriots who by and large safeguard their own culture, they have had to adjust to new invasions by pleasure seekers and English settlers. For no country, however fervently nationalistic, can today afford to proclaim itself an island.

The poet Robert Graves, who as a child explored the Harlech hills with his sisters, had this to say about the place in his autobiographical *Goodbye to All That* (first published in 1929):

> This country (and I know no country like it) seemed to be independent of formal nature. One hardly noticed the passage of the seasons there; the wind always blew across the stunted grass, the black streams always ran cold and clear, over black stones, the mountain sheep were wild and free, capable of scrambling over a six-foot wall . . . and, when in repose, easily mistaken for the lichen-covered granite boulders strewn everywhere. Few trees grew except hazels, rowans, stunted oaks and thorn bushes in the valleys. . . . Having no Welsh blood in us, we felt little temptation to learn Welsh, still less to pretend ourselves Welsh, but knew that country as a quite ungeographical region. . . . Had this been Ireland [the Graveses were part German, part Protestant Irish], we should have self-consciously learned Irish and local legends. . . . Instead we came to know Wales more purely as a place with a history too old for local legends; while walking there we made up our own. . . . On our visits to Germany I had felt a sense of home in a natural human way, but above Harlech I found a personal peace independent of history or geography. The first poem I wrote as myself concerned those hills.[2]

In 1986–87, when I first began to explore it, I responded to the Harlech landscape just as Graves had, before and during the First World War. The timelessness and placelessness of that country also, somehow, implies wordlessness. I don't know why slant light on coppery grass, spreading upward toward rounded, eroded, barren relics of the Ice Age moves me so much. But move me it does, so much so that it liberates me from a desire to explain myself. Such sights can mean more to people than their identities. Listen to another, quite different autobiographical passage, this time from *Period Piece,* a book of memoirs by the English artist Gwen Raverat. She is writing of the visits she paid as a child to Down House in Kent, home of her grandfather, Charles Darwin.

> The path in front of the veranda was made of large round water-worn pebbles, from some sea beach. They were not loose, but stuck down tight in moss and sand, and were black and shiny, as if they had been polished. I adored those pebbles. I mean literally, *adored;* worshipped. This passion made me feel quite sick sometimes. And it was adoration that I felt for the foxgloves at Down, and for the stiff red clay out of the Sandwalk clay-pit; and for the beautiful white paint on the nursery floor. This kind of feeling hits you in the stomach, and in the ends of your fingers, and it is probably the most important thing in life. Long after I have forgotten all my human loves, I shall still remember the smell of a gooseberry leaf, or the feel of the wet grass on my bare feet; or the pebbles in the path. In the long run it is this feeling that makes life worth living, this which is the driving force behind the artist's need to create.[3]

We generally think of writers as artists lucky enough to have exceptional facility with language. It may be, though, that such facility can be a handicap, for language as we understand it today looks to be more and more Janus-faced—that is to say, more and more untrustworthy as a system for conveying the kind of vital gut-feeling Gwen Raverat describes. A number of reasons for mistrusting contemporary language come to mind. Abstract words, for example, coined by the social sciences are too easily taken up by journalists or ideologists who need simple handles for their theories. In times like ours, with social change rampant and media communication so disproportionately influential, it may even be that our best, most sensitive writers are those *least* able to manipulate words, the *slowest* to fall into habits of convenience speech. Part of my purpose today is to draw attention to the way in which words, particularly words that stand for abstract generalizations, create beliefs: "The Way You Say the World Is What You Get"; not, you notice, what you "are" or what there "is," but what you—we all of us—"get" when we fall into the habit of constantly glossing the world with terminology.

Poets (in the broadest sense) have played many different roles throughout history, yet I can think of no time excepting the present when they have not in some sense been recognized as the chief custodians of language. Through language, writers have formed, guided, persuaded, and educated the public's often illiterate imagination—as Shelley proclaimed nearly two hundred years ago. And if today a vast audience, suspicious of high culture, identifies imagination with television advertising and the garish images continuously and ubiquitously jabbering on the small screen, that is hardly what Wallace Stevens or Robert Graves could have anticipated when, during the first half of this century, they concerned themselves—in quite different ways—with the complex relationship that exists between language and life. Or as Wallace Stevens has it, between imagination and reality.

Almost all Stevens's poems show—or attempt to show with a plethora of examples—that reality depends on our manner of conceiving it. In Stevens, creative imagination determines the worth of the world; and by implication, the more "reality" (he doesn't always use this word consistently) an individual creates, the richer life will be. Antithetical to individually creative acts are all ideological doctrines—religious, aesthetic, political—that publicly stifle free imagination. Once you cease to respond immediately to the world about you, once you substitute for experience some received mind-set or formula of belief, you yield up all the spontaneity and originality that renders life re-creatable as art. Look, for example, at the poem called "How to Live What to Do"—a sort of reversal of the Adam and Eve myth.

> Last evening the moon rose above this rock
> Impure upon a world unpurged.
> The man and his companion stopped
> To rest before the heroic height.
>
> Coldly the wind fell upon them
> In many majesties of sound:
> They that had left the flame-freaked sun
> To seek a sun of fuller fire.

Instead there was this tufted rock
Massively rising high and bare
Beyond all trees, the ridges thrown
Like giant arms among the clouds.

There was neither voice nor crested image,
Nor chorister, nor priest. There was
Only the great height of the rock
And the two of them standing still to rest.

There was the cold wind and the sound
It made, away from the muck of the land
That they had left, heroic sound
Joyous and jubilant and sure.[4]

Bare rock is a recurring symbol in Stevens, standing for the
world as given, what is "there" within and beneath and beyond
human imaginings. The "heroic" companions have escaped the
"flame-freaked sun" of religious art, say, in their search for some
truer, visionary sun. But all they find is "this tufted rock" un-
changed, for all its long past, by the unpurged "muck" of ideo-
logical belief. The rock's "heroic height" challenges them to
begin again, to create again a new aesthetic of human signifi-
cance. Note that the cold wind of reality in this poem is "joyous
and jubilant and sure." It offers the imagination nothing but
positive opportunity. In other poems—the famous "Snow Man,"
for example—Stevens makes it clear that nothingness, too, is a
concept that has to be imagined. But Stevens's rock is always a
place of possibility, a foundation for whatever meanings our
imaginations choose to create. And shared as such, it is invul-
nerable to assault by mortal despair—as also by greed, exploita-
tion, brutality, ugliness, meanness.

The whole body of Wallace Stevens's poetry (remember, he
belonged to the precomputer era) can be understood as an
aesthete's defense of art as the only sure way of knowing or
coming to terms with reality. His artists are heroes, whatever
their gender, who look straight at the speechless, ahuman world
in the light of the ahuman sun, and in participation with the
elements, imaginatively create meaning and beauty. Notice that
every creator, according to Stevens, is unique—a figure liber-
ated from accepted dogmas (the unpurged "muck of the land")
who deliberately chooses cultural isolation. You can see why

such an attitude enrages today's apostles of pluralism. And, indeed, Stevens's views do lay him open to criticism—if only because he never himself cut free from his own ideological aesthetic, or from the traditional cadences of English verse, or from the inherited Romanticism of the American tradition.

Yet Stevens—at his best—is one of America's most impressive, most moving poets. No one else has better described the strange excitement of creative experience; no one has written richer or more passionate poems about that experience; and no one has insisted with such credibility that the real artist always works with natural material at first hand. Though art is necessarily abstract, he implies, the abstracting must be done in a mind unencumbered by the expectations of a culture. In this respect, Stevens was not unlike that equally reclusive inhabitant of the rock, Emily Dickinson. Both poets outlived the ephemeral "muck" of their times, and they both speak, still, in their firmly individual voices.

In an essay called "The Noble Rider and the Sound of Words" Stevens contended that the purpose of poetry was to "help people live their lives."[5] Even if the person he helped most was himself—as he might have admitted—it is doubtful that he would have published without expecting that others would benefit. I don't suppose he anticipated that his poetry would help so many Ph.D. candidates to acquire doctorates, though it can't be denied that in that practical sense Stevens has indeed helped many people to live their lives. But surely, a shared sensibility means something else. It implies that individuals exist, that human souls are not merely products of genetic evolution and social acculturation; it implies that poetry can help people to find "the central" of their being, that it can nourish them and help them to be happy. Not all the time, of course, but sometimes. Consider these eight lines that introduce that epic-length meditation called "Notes towards a Supreme Fiction." The poet is addressing the spirit of poetry, an abstraction that in another poem he calls "the necessary angel of earth."

> And for what, except for you, do I feel love?
> Do I press the extremist book of the wisest man
> Close to me, hidden in me day and night?
> In the uncertain light of single, certain truth,

Equal in living changingness to the light
In which I meet you, in which we sit at rest,
For a moment in the central of our being,
The vivid transparency that you bring is peace.

The wordless experience those lines describe is close to mystical. Intimations of a like Presence can be found in the writings of Julian of Norwich, Thomas Traherne, George Herbert, T. S. Eliot, Edwin Muir, as also, I believe, in Wordsworth, Hopkins, and Whitman. Such an emotion is not uncommonly expressed by painters—for example, the passage I read earlier from Gwen Raverat's *Period Piece*. Stevens himself quotes from the musician Georges Enesco in an epigraph to a marvelous poem, "The World as Meditation."

J'ai passé trop de temps à travailler mon violon, à voyager. Mais l'exercice essentiel du compositeur—la méditation—rien ne l'a jamais suspendu en moi. . . . Je vis une rêve permanent, qui ne s'arrête ni nuit ni jour.

Paradoxically, it is in this abstract sense that an artist is enabled to represent his own time, and thus connect time with time through the medium of individual insight. "Poetry," Stevens once wrote, "is a process of the personality of the poet."[6] Isn't "personality"—he did not mean the self-regarding "I" of confessional verse—the key to every poet's identity? Between the poet and his or her writing a dialogue emerges, a quarrel with the self, as Yeats said, but enacted on a timeless stage, so it is *overheard* by an audience—of how many generations?—that can recognize and participate in it. The poet's obligation is to talk to himself, but that self is one that has been formed and informed over many years by a common language; and it is through that language again that the self dissolves and gives itself, with perhaps a name, to human time through the medium of a specific culture.

Recognizing the personal universality of poetry—the muse, "the necessary angel" of imagination—Stevens believed that no true poetry could be "programmed" to gratify specific political or social expectations. The recent experience of artists in the former Soviet Union surely justifies such a view. Any imaginative work of worth makes its values felt; it is not the poet's job to buttonhole readers or TV producers or prize givers. Stevens summed up his position in one of his last poems, "The Planet on the Table."

> Ariel was glad he had written his poems.
> They were of a remembered time
> Or of something seen that he liked.
>
> . . . .
>
> It was not important that they survive.
> What mattered was that they should bear
> Some lineament or character,
>
> Some affluence, if only half-perceived,
> In the poverty of their words,
> Of the planet of which they were a part.

For all Stevens's love of words—and no poet has relished more the sensuousness of his medium—it appears that, in the end, they were not enough. Ariel's imaginings, note, could at best only half-perceive reality "in the poverty of their words." It would be wrong, I think, to think of "affluence" here, or "poverty" in an economic context . . . as critics sometimes have. The matter in hand is metaphysical, and the implication? That reality is far, far greater than words can express. And although in many of his poems Stevens implies that the language of art alone can make us happy, toward the end of his life it seems he came closer to the position of Isaac Newton: human beings, in respect of the truth, are no more than children playing with pebbles on the seashore.

Notice again, though, how Stevens emphasizes the uniqueness of his vision. "His self and the sun were one"—not his self and his society were one. Though Wallace Stevens was not, like his Californian contemporary Robinson Jeffers, positively antisocial and "*un*humanist," it cannot escape anyone's notice that Stevens's landscapes are underpopulated, or that the characters who do appear in his poems—from the Emperor of Ice Cream to Mrs. Pappadopoulos[7]—are makeups or mock-ups invented to illustrate ideas. Such a deliberate withdrawal from social and historical contingency does, I think, limit the appeal of Stevens's poems, and it certainly puts many of them out of reach of readers for whom reality is *only* human, *only* cultural. So let's look at a poem by our more neglected friend Robert Graves, whose personal participation in human events was always much greater than Stevens's. Graves's poem is called "The Cool Web."

> Children are dumb to say how hot the day is,
> How hot the scent is of the summer rose,
> How dreadful the black wastes of evening sky,
> How dreadful the tall soldiers drumming by.
>
> But we have speech, to chill the angry day,
> And speech, to dull the rose's cruel scent.
> We spell away the overhanging night,
> We spell away the soldiers and the fright.
>
> There's a cool web of language winds us in,
> Retreat from too much joy or too much fear:
> We grow sea-green at last and coldly die
> In brininess and volubility.
>
> But if we let our tongues lose self-possession,
> Throwing off language and its watry clasp
> Before our death, instead of when death comes,
> Facing the wide glare of the children's day,
> Facing the rose, the dark sky and the drums,
> We shall go mad no doubt and die that way.[8]

A first response to "A Cool Web" might be that, for all its formal elegance, it's a strange poem for a poet to write. Instead of puffing up language, as poets usually do, Graves seems to disparage it. He reminds us that speech is a human construct—the protective cover into which people "retreat from too much joy or too much fear." Notice, too, the import of the first-person plural: "But *we* have speech, to chill the angry day." "Speech," then, is not here, as in Stevens, a uniquely creative medium; it gives no one special prerogatives to "make it new" on the planet's bare rock. Quite the contrary. Graves's cool web is common as water; language is the element in which human minds swim like fish. Without it, we would go mad and die. Especially take note of the double meaning of "spell": we spell words with letters, but we also weave spells, charms, out of words. I'm sure the ambiguity was intended.

Reality, for Graves, seems to have been a less confusing concept than for Stevens. Along with natural conditions—the hot day, the summer rose, the black wastes of evening sky—Graves cites, climactically in each of the first two stanzas, "the tall soldiers drumming by." Human reality, the poem implies, is most dangerous of all. Through language, through the propaganda of patriotism, we collectively permit ourselves to abjure responsibility for evil. During the Second World War, Wallace Stevens was fiercely attacked for escaping from civic responsibility into elitist aestheticism. It is likely, though, that he and Graves, along with Auden and Yeats, were, with respect to the politics of poetry, *au fond* in agreement. Remember what Yeats had to say in his disillusionment with the Republican struggle (which his friends supported) in Ireland.

> Hurrah for revolution and more cannon-shot!
> A beggar upon horseback lashes a beggar on foot.
> Hurrah for revolution and cannon come again!
> The beggars have changed places, but the lash goes on.[9]

Who, alas, will argue that it is not a natural propensity of humankind to gather into warring families, tribes, or classes motivated by self-interest? Or that in situations of war and social unrest individuals are not easily persuaded to depersonalize themselves (often by means of language) in the name of proclaimed beliefs—religious, ideological, political? I was about to write *denatured* for *depersonalized* when I realized that the word means just the opposite of what happens: in extremis, people, for the most part, are driven out of their civilized minds, back to their natural creature instincts. Correspondingly, the closer speech comes to public outcry, or to what Yeats termed rhetoric, the farther away it moves from reason and considered, individual response.

It could be argued that poets in the twentieth century, like their Romantic forebears of the nineteenth, have snared themselves in a double bind of language. Ever since Rousseau, pressure has been exerted to free poetry from reason, to persuade poets of their true affinity to nature—or to what amounts to the same thing, the irrational unconscious. Upon poets even more than upon psychiatrists has devolved the burden of finding language to express the inexpressible. Yet words, of their very essence, have to be *nonreal;* they can only express human forms of consciousness. That is their power and limitation—

surely what Graves was getting at in "The Cool Web." "There's a cool web of language winds us in," and that web embraces the "spells" of history, of organized religion, of psychoanalysis, of sociology, of philosophy, of politics, of economics—and also of poetry and fiction. For a writer to claim that he can free himself of "wrong" language by creating a new "right" one through the intensity of his imagination—as Wallace Stevens, in his charming way, seems to have done—suggests that he is indulging in too hopeful an illusion.

So Graves, with his cool web, undermines the Romantic underpinnings even of Stevens. "Children are dumb to say how hot the day is" suggests that children (before they can speak) suffer as animals suffer. We don't know how animals suffer; we like not to think about it, since we kill so many for our daily use. Even the world our pets feel lies outside our range. Who can describe what a dog smells, or what a cat senses with its whiskers? Similarly with a baby—as in Tennyson's *In Memoriam*—that has "no language but a cry."

Yet, however hard it is for poets to accept that reality is speechless, they are surely in a better position to say so than are politicians or journalists whose credibility depends not at all on truths they are unable to articulate but on reiterating public speech they can persuade people to believe. Many poets of the twentieth century, as you know, have in agony fought against the implications of Graves's insight. Latter-day romantics (mostly German or Austrian—Rainer Maria Rilke, Georg Trakl, Hermann Broch, and in philosophy Ludwig Wittgenstein) set a precedent for rejecting the treachery of words altogether and instead electing silence, madness, suicide over a humiliating submission to the cool web. The final silence of Sylvia Plath may be a case in point. In one of her last poems, "Words," she seems to be declaring, from the depth of suicidal depression, that language can do nothing to save her.

Any poet of the 1990s, then, confronts a debilitating dilemma. We inherit a tradition of English-language poetry that puts faith in words. The question of language's ultimate "truth" hardly arose until philosophical doubt, rising mainly out of the religious crisis of the mid–nineteenth century, pushed language toward the center of the debate. In at least nominally theocentric times, the question of man's place—and hence of language—in nature never arose. "In the beginning was the Word, and the Word was with God, and the Word was God" (John 1:1). For religions of the book—Christianity and Islam alike—the word still assumes divine authority, and man takes his rightful place in a fixed order of being.

Take God out of the picture, though, and put Homo sapiens in his place—as many, after Nietzsche (including, I suppose, Stevens) tried to do—and difficulties abound. And it is at this point, I think, that we must desert poetry for a while and call upon the natural sciences. For the crisis of the nineteenth century, as I understand it, was surely Darwinian before it was Nietzschean; and it was no part of evolutionary theory to substitute man or human imagination for God the Creator. It is a measure, perhaps, of the greatness of Darwin that he should have singled out man's "arrogance" as the troublesome obstacle. "Man in his arrogance," Darwin wrote in his notebooks, "thinks himself a great work, worthy the interposition of a deity, [it would be] more humble and I believe truer to consider himself created from animals."[10] If we were to consider language, also, in a more humble light, as evolved from animals over many thousands of years, we might perhaps gain a truer estimation of what it can and cannot tell us about reality.

What remains, then, for the poet committed to expressing reality but humbly distrustful of language? So far, in the years since the world wars, poetry in England and America has pretty well abandoned overarching problems of philosophical truth. There have been Freudian years and crisis years for the self (one thinks of Lowell's madness, Plath's, Berryman's, and Sexton's suicides). Today what is still called "poetry" in England and America has fragmented, for the most part, into a plethora of politically inspired factions. Instead of poetry in the English language we have black poetry, feminist poetry, gay poetry, working-class poetry, formalist poetry, and so on. The few poets who stand out from the crowd milling at the foot of Parnassus gain status from belonging to one or another social group. Derek Walcott is a West Indian; Seamus Heaney and Eavan Boland are Irish (everybody, it seems, loves the Irish); Tony Harrison speaks for the working class . . . and so forth. Of course, I don't mean that such poets are admired only for their political or racial status. Still, how many admirers readily drop poets' names who cannot recite a single line of their verse? In trying to articulate something of what I feel language is doing to us, I came up with the verses that gave me the title of this talk. Pushing on from Graves's "The Cool Web" (which I read for the first time only two summers ago), it depicts language as a two-way system, both of imagination and escape, and it includes within its scope the invitingly illusory dimension of television.

> The way you say the world is what you get.
> What's more, you haven't time to change or choose.
> The words swim out to pin you in their net
>
> Before you guess you're in the TV set
> Lit up and sizzling in unfriendly news.
> The mind's machine—and you invented it—
>
> Grinds out the formulae you have to fit,
> The ritual syllables you need to use
> To charm the world and not be crushed by it.
>
> This cluttered motorway, that screaming jet,
> Those crouching skeletons whose eyes accuse,
> O see and say them, make yourself forget
>
> The world is vaster than the alphabet
> And profligate, and meaner than the muse.
> A bauble in the universe? Or shit?
>
> Whichever way, you say the world you get.
> Though what there is is always there to lose.
> No crimson name redeems the poisoned rose;
> The absolute's irrelevant. And yet . . .

Stevens, whose poetry is more complicated than I have made out, believed that reality is created when the artist and the natural world combine to produce an image of it. Graves thought reality too dangerous, too alien to civilization to get into language at all. Plath eventually spurned the deceptive traps of words, choosing silence over compromise. And today, taking our cue about equally from advanced technology and historical guilt, masses of us have retreated from reality altogether into a fantasy that places human life—and theoretically every single person's human rights—at the epicenter of all matter. The more we explain ourselves, the more we define what we want and complain about what we haven't got, the more arrogant as human beings we tend to become. Or to put it aphoristically, the more we say the world we get, the more we get the world we say. We are all of us trapped in the mill, and language is the force that turns the wheel.

Yet that isn't my last word, either. For there are ways out; and for those of us fortunate enough to have time and inclination to give ourselves, rarely, to the ahuman, wordless world (as both Stevens and Graves did) there are wonders innumerable to be perceived. One of these ways—and I must of necessity be brief in suggesting it—is to pay attention to what contemporary science (rather than critical theory or poststructuralist philosophy) is coming up with. In a prologue to an introduction to *The Quantum Universe*, by Tony Hey and Patrick Walters, the late Richard Feynman had this to say.

> Poets say science takes away from the beauty of the stars—mere globs of gas atoms. Nothing is "mere." I too can see the stars on a desert night, and feel them. But do I see less or more? The vastness of the heavens stretches my imagination—stuck on this carousel, my little eye can catch one-million-year-old light [. . .] Or I can see [the stars] with the greater eye of Palomar, rushing all apart from some common starting point when they were perhaps all together. What is the pattern, or the meaning, or the why? It does not do harm to the mystery to know a little about it. For far more marvelous is the truth than any artists of the past imagined! Why do the poets of the present not speak of it?[11]

Once released from anthropocentric obsession, any poet, any observant person of whatever race or gender, can become, for moments anyway, that eye—*e-y-e*, not the ubiquitous capital *I*—to which nothing is "mere." In "The Cool Web" Graves represented nature—human and otherwise—as literally too terrifying for words, but in the future, self-cancellation (loosing yourself to find yourself) might well come to be accepted as a poet's necessary prerequisite for finding words to express something of what Feynman and others like him have discovered to be the most spiritual and miraculous challenge of reality.

NOTES

1. Robert Hughes, *Culture of Complaint: The Fraying of America* (New York: Oxford University Press), 1993.

2. Robert Graves, *Goodbye to All That* (London: Penguin Books, 1960), 34–35.

3. Gwen Raverat, *Period Piece* (London: Faber and Faber, 1952), 141–42.

4. All poems and excerpts from poems by Wallace Stevens reproduced in this essay can be found in *The Collected Poems of Wallace Stevens* (New York: Knopf, 1954).

5. Wallace Stevens, "The Noble Rider and the Sound of Words," in *The Necessary Angel* (New York: Vintage Books, 1953), 29.

6. Wallace Stevens, "The Figure of the Youth as Virile Poet," in *The Necessary Angel,* 45.

7. For Mrs. Pappadopoulos, see "So and So Reclining on Her Couch," *Collected Poems,* 295–96.

8. "The Cool Web," *Collected Poems (1914–1947)* (London: Cassell, 1948), 51.

9. W. B. Yeats, "The Great Day," in *Collected Poems of W. B. Yeats* (London: Macmillan, 1933), 358.

10. Adrian Desmond and James Moore, *Darwin, a Biography* (London: Penguin Books, 1992), 252.

11. Tony Hay and Patrick Walters, *The Quantum Universe* (Cambridge: Cambridge University Press, 1993), 1.

An Interview with Richard Poole

Anne, you divide your time between cottages in Grantchester and Cwm Nantcol. When I think of Grantchester I think of Rupert Brooke's famous poem, with its lilacs and roses, spectral dancing vicars and immortal river under the mill. Cwm Nantcol is as different from that as anywhere could be, with its rugged Cambrian rocks and wild goats. Which place best suits your temperament?

When I think of Grantchester, I think of nearby Cambridge, where I happen to have been born, where I first married, and where, if my premonition is right, I'll probably die. My toehold in Grantchester is like the long root that still hooks me to academia. Though I don't think too bookish an environment is good for poetry, my husband and I, in our different ways, are reading people. Grantchester represents the hard-thinking, plain-living, music-playing tradition in which I was raised. For Cambridge, read also Ann Arbor, Michigan, where I went to school and university.

Cwm Nantcol, in contrast, represents a retreat to a timeless, glacier-sculpted topography. Its ancient stumps of mountains have survived hundreds of millions of years of drifting across oceans, being folded in and out of land masses, carved and smoothed by ice age after ice age. The place puts us in our place. In bad weather its stormy blackness can weigh upon the spirit something awful. But when this Great Cwm, as the geologist Adam Sedgwick saw it, floods with sunlight, it's a dazzling green—or in the fall and winter, burnished copper. I know of no place like it. Being an up-and-down sort of person, I like up-and-down weather and landscapes.

Has Cwm Nantcol changed you in any way?

Not changed me. Confirmed, maybe, something I'd known and long forgotten. I'm reminded of a poem by Robert Frost I

From *Poetry Wales* 31, no. 4 (April 1996). Reprinted with permission.

learned by heart when I was about fifteen, "Into My Own." The poet imagines his return to his family and friends after a trip to "the edge of doom."

> They would not find me changed from him they knew.
> Only more sure of all I thought was true.

Your recent poems seem receptive to the long perspectives that modern science—geology, biology, physics—have opened up on ourselves and our tenancy of the planet. Do you see science as the poet's ally rather than enemy?

A bad habit we've acquired over the past two hundred years is that of separating *science*—knowledge—from *poetry,* a word derived from the Greek *poiein,* to make or create. The war between science and the arts probably flared up toward the end of the eighteenth century, in England at the time of Blake, when philosophical systems based on skepticism and abstract reasoning threatened the poets' delight in the mysterious. Wordsworth, though, in his preface to the *Lyrical Ballads,* looked forward to a time when "the poet will lend his divine spirit to the transfigurations" that he foresaw science bringing about. Today, science has immeasurably increased our sense of mystery, while it has certainly created a material world in which, with all other species, we teeter on a razor's edge between survival and destruction. I think it's important for poets now to follow Wordsworth's injunction and carry "sensation into the midst of Science itself." No myth, however much we pray, can ever again claim to be the literal truth. Poets should be showing us how to read myths metaphorically, as lessons in psychology, or as moral parables.

Scientists can express ideas about the universe in mathematical formulae. Poets must do it in language. Does language trap poets in an anthropomorphic bind? Must it prevent them, for example, from ever grasping the otherness of natural objects?

I'm no mathematician, but surely language and mathematics are two different ways of using symbols to communicate meaning. Mathematical formulae do express limited, irrefutable truths that words can't. That's probably why numbers have been held to be supernaturally powerful in the past. But then words can express so much else! What could be more narrowly binding to the spirit than the principles of logic, the form of language closest to mathematics? Poets worry, sometimes, because they are unable easily to understand mathematical proofs—at least, I worry. Yet I don't believe that astrophysicists and microbiologists "grasp the otherness of natural objects" any better than Robert Frost or Elizabeth Bishop did. Scientists contribute to human understanding in one way, poets in quite another. One of the poet's jobs is to bear witness to human emotions and human feelings. But scientists and poets alike are faced with the unfathomable mystery of existence.

*You have a poem called "The Way You Say the World Is What You Get."
David Wright said in "Words":*

> *Constructing from words the poem,
> I say what they say I should say
> Rather than what I would say. They
> Use us where we would use them.*

Is all poetic endeavor a compromise with a medium that has a mind of its own?

Well, that was Humpty Dumpty's problem: who shall be master. And Lewis Carroll deliberately made Humpty Dumpty ridiculous. No one can make a word mean "just what I choose it to mean" and succeed in everyday communicating. David Wright, like the Scottish poet W. S. Graham (both were wonderful poets), worried about the way language uses us. But their worry was really about society, about the way any culture uses language to influence individuals. And that's what I worry about, too. "The way you say the world is what you get" suggests that we live the way our culture tells us to. If the TV's there and you watch it, you accept its *terms,* even if you disagree with this or that program. The difference between the poet and the adman, for example, is not that the poet fights the language; he fights the misuse or overuse of words we hold in common. Since language is a tool, it has no will of its own, it's *always* manipulated—sometimes for good, sometimes for evil. Imagine a battle between a bad magician—a propagandist—who wants to bind or blind us with the power of words, and a good magician who wants to teach us to use them for our enlightenment.

Robert Graves's poem "The Cool Web" claims that language "winds us in" to protect us from the horrors of speechless nature. There's truth in that—*some* truth—though there's lots of speechless nature in Cwm Nantcol, and I, for one, find it a relief! My image of language is rather more domestic. Think of any language as a single sheet you are trying to fit on a big double bed. You no sooner cover one corner than the one opposite is laid bare. You manage to tuck it in at the top, but the bottom remains exposed. There is no way the language-sheet is going to cover the *whole* bed! So we have a choice. We can petulantly throw away the sheet and give up trying to express reality altogether. Or we can make do with a bed only half made-up. I myself would choose the latter.

You said in an essay published a few years ago in America that Cwm Nantcol is "an easy place to live in" because you cannot identify with the Welsh. Could you expand on that?

Living as we do among Welsh-speaking neighbors in Cwm Nantcol, my husband and I naturally feel ourselves to be foreigners. And let me add that neither of us have ever been made to feel personally uncomfortable because of this. Our Welsh neighbors couldn't be more friendly. My husband, though, is English, and insofar as I feel any country to be "home," it's America. I wouldn't say I was any sort of nationalist. Certainly not an imperialist! After what's been happening in Northern Ireland, Israel, and Bosnia, it's hard to see nationalism as the answer to many political problems. (That doesn't mean I'm for too much centralized government, either.) On the whole I tend to think of people as "real," while nations are historical creations. One historian, Benedict Anderson, defined a nation as an "imagined political community," giving full weight to the word *imagined*. Imagination can do wonderful things for people, and it can do terrible things. Like language. I feel happiest when I'm free of group pressures of all kinds. In Wales, we live in a *locality*, there's a community, if you like. But even the word *community* is tainted with political correctness these days.

In their different ways, American writers and what used to be called Anglo-Welsh writers worry a lot about identity. Is identity an issue for you?

Yes and no. *Identity* is a loaded word. I try to avoid it. We used to have souls, after Freud we had psyches, and now we have identities. I think it's important not to take ourselves too seriously. None of us can be individually sacred. Although we human beings are precious to ourselves and sometimes (not always!) to each other, from nature's point of view we have to be dispensable.

A poem called "Trinity at Low Tide" in your most recent collection, Four and a Half Dancing Men, *seems to offer a meditation on identity. The poem's second-person focus accompanies a shadow and a reflection in a walk down "a glassy beach."*

> *Under you, transparent yet exact,*
> *your downward ghost keeps pace—*
> *pure image, cleansed of human overtones:*
> *a travelling sun, your face;*
> *your breast a field of sparkling shells and stones.*
> *All blame is packed into that black, featureless*
> *third trick of light that copies you*
> *and cancels you.*

These different effects of the light propose different versions of the self—one light, one dark. I'm not at all sure how to read the tone of the closing cancellation, however; one minute it seems detached, the next resentful. Can you look on your own cancellation with equanimity?

At certain times effacement seems attractive; Sylvia Plath invoked it a good deal. When I wrote "Trinity at Low Tide" I believed it was playful, a light meditation on the three-in-one I actually *saw* as my husband walked "sole to sole" with his reflection at ebb tide along Harlech Beach, with his shadow stalking beside him. You can read it in a number of ways; for instance, your subjective "self" is not the "you" other people recognize, nor is it the corporeal object that nature created. We are most of us a number of things at once, depending on point of view, depending on the "light" in which we're viewed.

In another poem, "Painting It In," you wrote about the experience of being enclosed in one of those thick Welsh mountain mists. The poem concludes unexpectedly:

> *Hills, stones, sheep, trees are, as yet, impossible.*
> *And when things are unmade, being also feels less alone.*

Conventional wisdom would have it that the opposite is the case—that it's the presence of things around us that connects us to the world. Are you being deliberately provocative here?

I didn't mean to be. I had in mind something like the Christian mystics' "Cloud of Unknowing"—a good feeling I often have, and not only in a Welsh mist, of losing the sense of myself and dissolving into something much larger. One experiences a similar sense of otherness when one reads very intensely. Wallace Stevens's poem "The House Was Quiet and the World Was Calm" beautifully describes such a moment: "The reader became the book; and summer night / Was like the conscious being of the book." One of the great poems.

To what extent are poems, for you, made out of ideas, and to what extent out of experiences?

I don't know. Is there really a distinction? Ideas *are* experiences. You might say, even, that no experience can be written down unless it rises into consciousness as an idea. Hence the enormous importance of imagination. Imagination is in*form*ed or re*form*ed memory. Not only in words; equally so in images and, for many, including myself, in music. Of course, we have experiences all the time that we don't name, as dogs and cats do (or so we assume). A poem arrives when words somehow flock to an experienced occasion. A phrase, like a line of music, presents itself and challenges the poet to carry it on. Rarely do poems write themselves. They come in dribs and drabs, and often a formal structure of stanzas or syntax helps the poet to "make" a poem. In most cases, the poem made does not coincide exactly with the experience that set it going. I tried to say this in "An Unfinished Poem."

> In the event
> the event is sacrificed
> to a fiction of its having happened . . .

But I don't as a rule think abstract ideas alone lend themselves to poetry. I rarely write a poem that is wholly idea (as Wallace Stevens sometimes did). On the other hand, I almost never simply describe or emote.

Recently you've been putting together a collected poems for OUP. Was selecting what to put in and what to leave out a difficult task?

Not really. I enjoyed going over my old books, sometimes thinking "Why, that wasn't so bad! How did I ever do that at the age of thirty?" Again, some poems that used to be important to me wouldn't do at all; they seemed terrible. Like other poets, though, I'm vain. I like to think I've done my best over the years.

Did you feel the need to revise early poems? Mightn't revising the poems of one's youth . . . constitute a violation of their naïveté?

Yes, I did revise, but in most cases revision was a simple matter of excising chunks from longer poems. If I hadn't cut them I wouldn't have printed them. A long meditation called "England," for instance, written in 1966, seems interesting as an evocation of an England that hardly exists in 1996. I wanted to retain it, but I had to chop some embarrassing bits out. The title poem of "Travelling behind Glass"—about a woman changing in a country that is itself changing—never did end to my satisfaction. I made another stab—the umpteenth—at finishing the last page, and it now seems better, not perfect. Wasn't it Valéry who said that a poem is never finished, only abandoned?

Some years ago Bitter Fame, *your biography of Sylvia Plath, proved to be extremely controversial. You were denounced by some reviewers who thought your unflattering portrait of Plath unacceptable. Were you surprised at the vehemence of the response?*

I suppose I was naive, but I was surprised that, having labored to produce a fair book, I was denounced for reasons that had little to do with the biography in hand. I probably shouldn't have taken it on, but Plath was a challenge. She was exactly my age, yet when I began cautiously to publish in 1965, she was already dead and famous. She and Anne Sexton, powerful word-witches that they were, turned poetry into a particularly dangerous type of psychodrama. I wrote *Bitter Fame* principally to show how risky it is to indulge in the saga of your own myth, casting yourself as a doomed heroine. For some time Sylvia Plath pulled me into her orbit. I hope my *Collected Poems* will demonstrate the measures I took to escape from it. Plath poses no threat to me now, of course. She strikes me as tragically young, still trapped in her wunderkind adolescence. I came to feel very sorry for her. I don't think my book is unsympathetic to her, either.

Reading reviews of women writers by other women writers, I sometimes detect the presence of a certain kind of feminist political correctness. Here in Wales, for instance, Sheenagh Pugh is sometimes criticized for "masculine" traits of mind. Have you experienced this sort of pressure?

Good for Sheenagh Pugh! I can't imagine paying court to any sort of political correctness. The bane of the age! If women and men can't share "traits of mind" as well as jobs and role definitions, I don't want anything to do with feminism. I dislike isms. All this political correctness nonsense smacks of what my husband aptly calls "post-Communist conformism." As you may have deduced from what has gone before, I'm a "teeth-gnashing liberal individualist"—as a publican acquaintance of mine in Hay used to say of himself.

You were recently in conversation with Germaine Greer at the National Theatre in London. Are you sympathetic to her criticism of female academics who want to rewrite the canon to include a host of women writers only they have heard of?

I admire Germaine Greer's *Slipshod Sibyls* as much as any book I've read this year; it takes pride of place with Ted Hughes's *Winter Pollen*. Yes, it seems to me as ridiculous to study women's bad poetry as men's. There's no point in resurrecting forgotten writing of the past unless it's pretty good as art; or historically interesting, as *Slipshod Sibyls* shows us some of it is. I have no objections to questioning "the canon," as it's glibly called. I'm sure there's a great deal of buried stuff that merits attention. But it does seem silly to judge poetry purely on grounds of gender.

Here's a tough one. Does contemplation of the state of poetry writing and publishing in Britain at the moment fill you with satisfaction, alarm, or despair?

Oh, I feel very old these days, and the old always despair of the young. What with the deconstructionist model on one hand and the populist political one on the other, I worry that talented younger poets are falling between two stools. It may take several decades for a major poet to emerge. Or it may be that poetry, as the word used to be understood, is obsolete and will never again be wanted. The best poetry of the future may be dramatic, written for television. And why not? Poetry ought to be as accessible to sensitive, alert people as prose fiction. It shouldn't ever have become the property of an academic elite.

As to the *quantity* produced, poetry is certainly thriving, in Wales as all over Britain. You could say that poetry is now a genuinely popular art-form, and that wouldn't be a bad thing if most of it were genuinely poetry. Really, I suppose I'm in despair, not with poetry—there's gold, still, in the dross—but with the general state of British culture. It seems to me at once degenerate and self-congratulatory; mediocrity crowning mediocrity at every possible level; and the whole prizefight sponsored by well-meaning bureaucrats.

If you were asked to advise a young would-be poet on whom to read of twentieth-century poets, what names would you come up with?

If there is one thing I've learned over many years of "teaching" poetry, it's never to recommend a living poet to the aspiring young. Let them tell you what they read! That will give you a clue to what they're up to . . . or not up to, if they happen never to read poetry by anybody but themselves. Of late I've found it useful to keep what I call "The Ongoing Anthology." Whenever I find a poem I admire, whether in a book or magazine, I copy it on my word processor, print it out, and collect it in a loose-leaf folder. (In former days I would have copied it by hand into a notebook, but why not make the most of modern technology?) Leafing through it, I see there's a good deal of Shakespeare, Herbert, and Blake—it's nothing if not canonical! But from the twentieth century, among other poems, here's Yeats's "Among School Children"; Frost's "Home Burial" and "The Most of It"; Auden's "The Shield of Achilles"; Louis MacNeice's "Prayer before Birth" and "House on a Cliff"; Elizabeth Bishop's two sestinas, together with "The Moose" and "Roosters"; Richard Wilbur's "Love Calls Us to the Things of This World"; sections from Eliot's *Four Quartets;* Wallace Stevens's "Anecdote of the Jar," "The Snow Man," "The House Was Quiet," and "The World as Meditation"; Seamus Heaney's "The Harvest Bow" and "Strange Fruit"; parts of Gillian Clarke's "Letter from a Far Country"; Derek Mahon's "In Carrowdore Churchyard"; Ted Hughes's "Horses"; some of Derek Walcott's "Omeros"; R. S. Thomas's "A Marriage"—and yes, Sylvia Plath's "Candles" and "Words" and four pages of Larkin. But I could name at least fifty twentieth-century poets to whose work I continually return. Perhaps the best rule is to talk poems, not poets. Poets live too much in each other's pockets, anyway. The best poems always outlive their makers.